THE STATESMAN
AS THINKER

THE STATESMAN AS THINKER

PORTRAITS OF GREATNESS, COURAGE, AND MODERATION

DANIEL J. MAHONEY

ENCOUNTER BOOKS   NEW YORK · LONDON

First American edition published in 2022 by Encounter Books,
an activity of Encounter for Culture and Education, Inc.,
a nonprofit, tax-exempt corporation.
Encounter Books website address: www.encounterbooks.com

Manufactured in the United States and printed on
acid-free paper. The paper used in this publication meets
the minimum requirements of ANSI/NISO Z39.48—1992
(R 1997) (*Permanence of Paper*).

FIRST AMERICAN EDITION

LIBRARY OF CONGRESS CATALOGING-IN-PUBLICATION DATA

Names: Mahoney, Daniel J., 1960- author.
Title: The statesman as thinker : portraits of greatness, courage, and
moderation / Daniel J. Mahoney.
Description: First American Edition. | New York : Encounter Books, 2022.
Includes bibliographical references and index.
Identifiers: LCCN 2021042455 (print) | LCCN 2021042456 (ebook)
ISBN 9781641772419 (Hardcover : acid-free paper) | ISBN 9781641772426 (eBook)
Subjects: LCSH: Political leadership–Case studies.
Political ethics–Case studies. | Cardinal virtues. | Magnanimity.
Burke, Edmund, 1729-1797–Political and social views.
Tocqueville, Alexis de, 1805-1859–Political and social views.
Lincoln, Abraham, 1809-1865–Political and social views.
Churchill, Winston, 1874-1965–Political and social views.
Gaulle, Charles de, 1890-1970–Political and social views.
Havel, Václav–Political and social views.
Classification: LCC JC330.3 .M25 2022 (print) | LCC JC330.3 (ebook)
DDC 303.3/4–dc23/eng/20220111
LC record available at https://lccn.loc.gov/2021042455
LC ebook record available at https://lccn.loc.gov/2021042456

1 2 3 4 5 6 7 8 9 20 22

CONTENTS

INTRODUCTORY NOTE:
'THERE IS VIRTUE IN THE GAZE
OF A GREAT MAN'

In one of the greatest prose works of French literature, *Memoirs from Beyond the Tomb*, François-René de Chateaubriand (universally known as Chateaubriand) draws a most artful, instructive, and memorable comparison between George Washington and Napoleon Bonaparte. Chateaubriand was a Legitimist (a supporter of the old French monarchy in the form of the Bourbon family), a Catholic, and what one might call an aristocratic liberal, a profound lover and defender of human freedom and dignity (and also a romantic when it came to things of the heart). He had no trouble discerning Napoleon's greatness, but he came to see that it was bereft of goodness and of a genuine concern for the common good. He irrevocably broke with Napoleon after the kidnapping and eventual execution of the Duc d'Enghien on March 21, 1804, seeing in this cruel and cold act a terrible crime that "introduced a new principle into Bonaparte's conduct."[1] Henceforth, Bonaparte

---

1 All quotations from Chateaubriand's *Memoirs from Beyond the Tomb*, selected and translated by Robert Baldick (London and New York: Penguin Books, 1961 and 2014), are cited internally and parenthetically in the body of the text as *MFBTT* followed by the appropriate page number.

became "an object of fear and suspicion." His soul was sullied, and he became more openly and coldly despotic: "His great qualities remained the same, but his good dispositions became impaired and no longer supported his great qualities; corrupted by that original stain, his nature deteriorated" (*MFBTT*, 221). Reflecting on the fall of Napoleon first in 1814 and then after the Battle of Waterloo in 1815, Chateaubriand castigated the selective memory of too many of the French people who only remembered Napoleon's glory but could not "hear the curses of [his] victims and their cries of pain and distress." In the end, the French as a whole became "weary of his tyranny and his conquests" (*MFBTT*, 267). As Charles de Gaulle would later suggest, Napoleon is an object lesson in what happens when grandeur is separated from moderation.

To be sure, French circumstances made it difficult for Napoleon to play the role of Washington, but they did not necessitate endless conquests, the wholesale repression of political liberty, and the betrayal of his allies and admirers such as Tsar Alexander of Russia. Washington, whom Chateaubriand met on two occasions in Philadelphia in 1791, showed another more genuine path to greatness. He was the dignified president of a decent and lawful modern republic, one whose example revealed that "in order to be free, a man is no longer obliged to plough his own small field, to curse the arts and sciences, or to have hooked nails and a dirty beard" (*MFBTT*, 132), a playful response to Rousseau if there ever was one. Chateaubriand saw in Washington an antique grandeur, a Roman simplicity, and a remarkable example of a "soldier-citizen" (*MFBTT*, 133) who knew when to go home. When Chateaubriand met Washington in 1791, the French writer and diplomat had acquired little fame. Still, he felt "fortunate indeed" that the great man's "gaze should have fallen upon" him. He strikingly adds: "There is virtue in the gaze of a great man" (*MFBTT*, 134).

Chateaubriand later notes that when Washington went back to his estate at Mount Vernon in 1797 after two terms as president of the new American republic, he "cannot have experienced the regrets" that haunted Napoleon in exile. Chateaubriand goes to the heart of things: in the end, Napoleon was "a solitary man, he was sufficient unto himself, misfortune did nothing but to restore him to the desert that was his life" (*MFBTT*, 292). The tyrant, not the statesman, is marked in the end by a hollow if self-aggrandizing soul.

We must remember that Napoleon was no Lenin, Hitler, or Stalin, and he did not war on civilization as such. If Washington, like Churchill, was an "indomitable and magnanimous statesman," Napoleon was not what Leo Strauss rightly called Hitler, an "insane tyrant"[2] (with clear emphasis on moral insanity, not mental illness). Yet Bonaparte revealed the false allure of greatness shorn of the cardinal virtues first discerned by the ancients and further developed by Christian thought: courage, prudence, justice, and temperance. These virtues, and not the pursuit of power-seeking as an end in itself, are at the core of authentic political greatness.

The first chapter of this book, "Statesmanship as Human Excellence," serves as a synoptic introduction to the themes of the book as a whole and can profitably be read on its own terms. The book brings together two principal themes and emphases: the study of genuinely reflective and even philosophically minded statesman who embodied magnanimity, greatness of soul—marked by moderation, a public-spirited concern for the public good, and genuine depth of soul—with an analysis and articulation of the cardinal virtues that animate this rare combination of magnanim-

---

2 See Leo Strauss's "Remarks on Hearing of the Death of Churchill," January 25, 1965. These remarks form an epigraph to Harry V. Jaffa, editor, *Statesmanship* (Durham, NC: Carolina Academic Press, 1981), p. v.

ity and moderation. The qualities and virtues of such statesman are ably summarized by the nineteenth-century American Catholic man of letters Orestes Brownson: "What is especially needed in statesmen is public spirit, intelligence, foresight, broad views, manly feelings, wisdom, energy and resolution."[3] At its peaks, such rare but indispensable statesmanship is characterized by an unforced melding of the moral and intellectual virtues with a resoluteness and determination that steels those committed to the defense of ordered liberty and the inheritance that is civilization itself. Such, in fact, are the heroes of Western civilization. This study is intended to revive not just their memory but the understanding of what they represent.

This book is an exercise in what my friend the German Voegelinian political philosopher Tilo Schabert has called "empirical political philosophy" with a strong admixture of political history and even theological reflection. The empiricism Schabert and I refer to is not reductively positivistic, looking at only what can be quantified. No, it takes into account all the powers of the human soul and the wisdom—practical and intuitive or noetic— that transcends pragmatic rationality and the distorting identification of the real with only those things that can be measured in a very precise way. It is political science in the tradition of Aristotle and Tocqueville. The book does not aim to be exhaustive: It centers around Cicero, Burke, Washington, Tocqueville, Lincoln, Churchill, de Gaulle, and Havel while making collateral reference to Solon, Pericles, Jefferson, Pyotr Stolypin, Mandela, Reagan, and Thatcher. Its emphasis is on those rare and admirable souls who embodied magnanimity tempered by modera-

---

3 Cited by Kenneth Deutsch in his essay "Introduction: What is Statesmanship?" in Joseph R. Fornieri, Kenneth L. Deutsch, and Sean Dutton, editors, *American Statesmanship: Principles and Practice of Leadership* (Notre Dame, IN: University of Notre Dame Press, 2021), pp. 3–4.

tion, who embodied the cardinal virtues in a morally serious and realistic way, and whose rare combination of thought and action partook of the philosophical. All of this will be developed in a more fulsome and concrete way in Chapter 1. In a "Final Note," I will touch, but only touch, on more contemporary figures and developments.

This book is dedicated to the memory of the late great Roger Scruton, a true *defensor civitatis*, a learned, humane, and courageous opponent of every effort to negate human greatness and goodness in all its forms. Deepest thanks go to Philippe Bénéton, Pierre Manent, Giulio de Ligio, Ralph Hancock, and Paul Seaton, precious interlocutors on all things related to politics, philosophy, and the human soul. Geoffrey Vaughan read every chapter and provided very good advice and expert editing. I am indebted to a true friend and colleague. Gabrielle Maher provided invaluable help with typing and various organizational matters. My old and dear friend Jack Fowler provided constant encouragement along the way. Karen Wright, Tom Rastin, Richard Spencer, Dale and Wendy Brott, Peter J. Travers, and David Bahnsen provided crucial financial support that freed up more time to pursue this book project. Heartfelt thanks to all of them. Once again Roger Kimball of Encounter Books showed a generous openness to unfashionable ideas (such as political greatness) that our doctrinaire egalitarians so easily dismiss as hagiography and hero worship—and worse. Encounter and her sister enterprise, the indispensable cultural review *The New Criterion*, lead the way in putting liberal learning and culture at the service of true understanding and the defense of the ordered liberty at the heart of our civilized inheritance. Like Roger Scruton himself, they refuse to succumb to "the culture of repudiation" all around us.

I also would like to thank the editors of *Modern Age*, the *Cla-*

remont Review of Books, *The New Criterion*, *City Journal*, *The Political Science Reviewer*, and *Law and Liberty* for the opportunity to first develop some of these thoughts in their very fine journals and intellectual venues. We happy few...

Daniel J. Mahoney
Worcester, Massachusetts
August 7, 2021

STATESMANSHIP AS
HUMAN EXCELLENCE

The founding fathers of modern republicanism had no
qualms about appealing to the crucial role of the "founder" or "legislator" in establishing and sustaining free and lawful
political communities. The American founders, for example, read
their Cicero and Plutarch and were no doubt inspired by the accounts of political nobility found in the pages of both immensely
influential thinkers and writers. Their own noble deeds partake
of classical greatness of soul as much as the purported "realism"
of distinctively modern political thought. But it is undoubtedly
the case that they aimed to establish political institutions where
"power checked power," institutions that would make political
greatness less necessary if not superfluous. Is this one reason why
the study of statesmanship has fallen on hard times? Were they
too successful?

Perhaps statesmanship of the noblest and truest kind has always
been associated with crises of one sort or another: Solon addressing civil strife and class conflict in Athens in the sixth century
BC; Pericles steering a middle path between imperial grandeur

and prudent restraint in resisting the expansion of the Athenian Empire at the beginning of the Peloponnesian War; Cicero using all the arts of rhetoric and statesmanship in an ultimately failed attempt to save the remnants of Roman republicanism from the threat of Caesarian despotism; Burke eloquently warning defenders of ordered liberty against the proto-totalitarianism of Jacobin France; Washington leading the American people to their rightful station among the peoples of the earth and governing the new republic with an austere republican dignity; Lincoln preserving the Union and putting an end to the evil of chattel slavery at the same time; Churchill eloquently and firmly defending liberty and law and all the achievements of the "English-speaking peoples" against the dreadful barbarism of Nazism. Such statesmanship is, always and everywhere, a rare political achievement and an equally infrequent if admirable manifestation of the highest possibilities of the human soul.

Classical authors were right to understand such statesmanship as an elevated standard against which all political action can be judged. The thoughtful or reflective statesman exercises what the contemporary French political philosopher Pierre Manent calls "commanding practical reason," not arbitrary power or a plan to satisfy the lowest impulses of his soul. Every political community needs such commanding practical reason, an authoritative exercise of judgment and foresight at the service of the common good. But the doctrinaire egalitarianism and relativism that many today confuse with democracy do not readily allow for such qualitative differences to be acknowledged and affirmed.

Elementary distinctions "natural" to political life—the distinctions between authority and authoritarianism, reason and will, nobility and baseness, domination and the mutual accountability inherent in free political life—are effaced in the name of a terrible simplification. Arguments about "the advantageous and the just," as Aristotle so memorably put it in the opening chapters of his *Politics,* are summarily reduced to mere struggles for "power." This effacement of politics as a moral science goes hand in hand with a toxic egalitarian moralism that feels free to repudiate our civilized inheritance and to judge all thought and action in the light of the overlapping determinisms of "race, class, and gender." In truth, there can be no authentic political sphere, no veritable "public space," when thought and action are reduced to cruel and inexpiable struggles for power and domination. And whatever the antinomian left claims, the messianic struggle for "justice" will lead only to mayhem, violence, and tyranny if the goods of life are said to have no foundation in the human soul or the natural order of things. One cannot promote justice on the "willful" premises of Machiavellian (and Nietzschean) modernity. If one begins with nihilistic premises, if one reduces every argument to a pretense for domination and exploitation, one necessarily ends with the self-enslavement of man. A barely concealed nihilism cannot provide a foundation for common humanity, the civic common good, or mutual respect and accountability. In the end, it can only negate our civilized inheritance despite the perfectionist or utopian veneer that invariably accompanies it.

True and False Realism

Modern political philosophy and modern social science thus veer incoherently between false realism and an idealism that acknowledges no constraints on the power of the human will to remake human nature and society. Through sinuous but logical paths, modern realism gives way to a totalitarian assault on the very "givenness" of the human condition, an assault on human nature itself and on all the virtues that define the well-ordered soul. What is needed is a return to true realism, to a moral conception of politics that is fully realistic but that also acknowledges that the good, the search for legitimate authority or even the best regime, the exercise of the practical virtues—courage, moderation, prudence, and justice—are as real as, and certainly more ennobling and humanizing than, the reckless and groundless pursuit of power as an end in itself. As the French anti-totalitarian political thinker Raymond Aron wrote in his 1965 book, *Democracy and Totalitarianism*, Machiavellian "realism," in both its original and vulgarized forms, is imbued with a hidden or unacknowledged "metaphysic" that dogmatically reduces the philosophy, ideas, and justifications at the heart of real politics to an underlying will to power that alone is said to really move the souls of men. In this view, "The merits of a political *formula* do not lie in its worth or its truth, but in its usefulness. Ideas are merely weapons, methods of combat used by men engaged in the battle; but in battle the only goal is to win."

Aron wryly observes that "to decree that man is a futile plaything of his passions is no less philosophical than to give a meaning to human existence." Aron essentially endorses a phenomenological approach to the study of political things, one that does not assume without critical examination that the "essence of politics" can be found in an undifferentiated "struggle for power." A truly phenomenological approach to the study of politics and statecraft rejects both cynicism and dogmatism, according to Aron. Unlike the "false realists" who are "obsessed by the struggle for power," the true realist does not neglect another aspect of reality: "the search for legitimate power, for recognized authority, for the *best* regime." Such a student of politics fully appreciates the rough and tumble of political life, but he or she doesn't reduce it simplistically and dogmatically to an all-encompassing struggle for power. In *Democracy and Totalitarianism*, Aron gets to the heart of the matter:

> Men have never thought of politics as exclusively defined by the struggle for power. Anyone who does not see that there is a "struggle for power" element is naïve; anyone who sees nothing but this aspect is a false realist. The reality that we study is a human one. Part of this human reality is the question relating to the legitimacy of authority.

Aron's own study of political sociology, of comparative political regimes and ideologies, ultimately owes more to Montesquieu and Tocqueville, or to Aristotle, than to the power politics advocated in distinctive but complementary ways by both Machiavelli, at the beginning of the sixteenth century, and Max Weber, at the beginning of the twentieth (even if Aron was a serious and sometimes sympathetic student and scholar of both thinkers).

Let us now turn to the Roman statesman and political philosopher Cicero, whose thoughts and deeds provide much ballast for a morally serious and authentically realistic political science that avoids the twin temptations of dogmatism and cynicism and that remains firmly attentive to the virtues and goods that give life to free and decent politics. Cicero's moral realism provides an ample and accurate account of the motives at the heart of true statesmanship; the false realism that dominates modern or "Machiavellian" political science can only explain away what decent men and women cannot help but admire. What is needed today is not a return to classical politics per se but an openness to the judicious mix of realism and moral aspiration that informed the classical political philosophies of Aristotle and Cicero in particular. Unlike Plato, whose paramount theme was the superiority of the theoretical life, Aristotle and Cicero saw in statesmanship informed by political philosophy the highest practical human way of life, at once good for the soul and good for the city. They are philosophical partisans of statesmanship and political nobility par excellence.

Cicero's Model of the Magnanimous Statesman

The recovery of the dignity of the political vocation, of the distinction between the arbitrary exercise of power and honorable ambition that serves the common good, depends upon the restoration of distinctions that have been obfuscated by modern political philosophy and modern social science. As Cicero noted in the first book of *On Duties* (written in 44 BC, shortly before his death at the hands of Mark Antony), certain philosophers destroy the moral grounds of statesmanship by undermining the intrinsic link between the highest goods for human beings and the exercise of the moral and intellectual virtues. If vulgar pleasure or shameless self-seeking or even a more high-minded identification of philosophy with refined pleasure becomes the great desideratum, there is no reason for a citizen, statesman, or human being to "cultivate friendship, justice, or liberality." Power and pleasure become the exclusive ends and means of human and political life, and the distinction between the honorable statesman and the rapacious tyrant is eliminated in one fell swoop. This is one reason why Cicero despised the Epicureans, whose reduction of the good to the pleasant encouraged an abdication of moral and political responsibility on the part of the one, the few, and the many. If a thinker or leader—or citizen for that matter—identifies pain as "the greatest ill" and pleasure as "the greatest good," he has no reason to be brave or courageous or to make sacrifices for his country.

As Mary Ann Glendon has well put it, Cicero was that rare political man who combined "the noble sort of ambition with…intense attraction to the *eros* of the mind." He was at once a statesman and a moral and political philosopher even if he generally turned to writing his philosophical works when his "political fortunes were at a low ebb." His writings defend both the indispensability of philosophical reflection and the greatness of spirit inherent in noble statesmanship. He sometimes suggested that the life of the statesman informed by philosophy and right reason was the highest vocation open to human beings. However, "The Dream of Scipio," at the end of Cicero's *Republic*, with its reminder of the ultimate insignificance of human things from the perspective of the cosmos as a whole, seems to point in a rather different direction. In any case, Cicero, more than Plato and Aristotle, provides the most substantial and elevated argument for the inherent choice-worthiness of the life of the thoughtful and reflective statesman who combines greatness of soul with moderation and self-control. Cicero's beau ideal of a statesman is opposed to all narrow partisanship, which sunders the unity of the political community and, in extremis, can lead to civil war and to self-seeking at the expense of the common good.

The true statesman for Cicero embodies in the depths of his soul what tradition calls the cardinal virtues—courage, temperance, prudence, justice—as well as a commitment to political liberty or self-government and a principled and passionate opposition to the negation of civilized life that is tyranny in its various forms. Cicero's statesman as thinker prefers peace to war, magnanimity to peevish resentment, clemency to the perpetual aggravation of the hatreds and divisions that destroy the moral integrity of the civic community. But if he prefers peace to war—domestic courage to martial courage, as Cicero calls it—if he appreciates that in the best circumstances arms should "yield to the toga," he is no pacifist or advocate of peace at any price. Themistocles, who saved Athens against Xerxes and the Persians at the Battle of Salamis in 480 BC, is rightly esteemed. But Solon, who gave Athens decent laws that safeguarded the rights and prerogatives of both the rich and the poor, the few and the many, "must be judged no less superb than the former." "Honorable conduct" reflects strength of spirit far more than strength of body, a cultivation of "urbane affairs" over "martial ones." In a republic in the process of being transformed into an empire, in a political culture that valued military prowess and heroism above all, Cicero reminded his readers that war was never an end in itself but an instrument to be used prudently and justly, if at all possible, to safeguard the achievements of a free and civilized political order. To rashly turn to battle, to unthinkingly prefer war to peace, "befits a certain savagery and is similar to brutes."

Still, Cicero reminds us, "when circumstance and necessity demand, we must physically fight it out to the end, preferring death to slavery and disgrace." An honorable statesman, "a truly magnanimous and courageous man," should prefer "affability" and "high-mindedness" to "useless and hateful peevishness." But Cicero acknowledged that "gentleness and clemency must be commended only as far as severity may also be employed for the sake of the commonwealth." Cicero's honorable statesman is equally distant from the amoral self-assertion of the Nietzschean "Overman," contemptuous as he is of his inferiors and from the deep aversion to the legitimate exercise of authority by the contemporary humanitarian. His standard is the "*honestum*"—the fine, the noble, the honorable—at the service of civilized liberty. He resists the siren calls of both hardness—tyranny, cruelty, and an immoral power politics—and softness, which is tenderness, compassion, or generosity bereft of any deep understanding of human nature or of the "inventiveness of wickedness," as Edmund Burke once so suggestively called it.

Half-classical modern democratic statesmen such as Charles de Gaulle and Winston Churchill embodied important aspects of this Ciceronian ideal. Their examples both vivify and illustrate this ideal and reveal it to be an enduring model of humane and tough-minded statecraft. They lived in an era strikingly different from Cicero's. In the first half of the twentieth century, modern technology and totalitarian ideologies made total war a real possibility, while creature comforts and a democratic ideology at the service of enlightenment, progress, and cosmopolitanism made pacifism a much more powerful temptation. Christianity had undoubtedly softened mores, quite significantly in the long run, even if it strengthened sectarian animosities during the wars of religion. A debilitating relativism that accompanied modern thought weakened the clear-cut distinctions between civilization and barbarism, freedom and totalitarianism. As Churchill noted in *The Gathering Storm*, the first volume of *The Second World War*, democracies had a difficult time cultivating and sustaining a coherent policy or strategy for even a relatively modest period of time. So, in a late modern world tempted by passivity, pacifism, and humanitarian illusions, the Ciceronian statesman must spend as much time warning against pacifist illusions as in reminding warrior republics of the ultimate superiority of the urbane virtues to military courage. The ideal remains the same: greatness tethered to measure, action informed by high prudence (as opposed to mere calculation), the moral virtues at the service of the civic common good, action informed by prudent reflection and a coherent vision of the well-ordered soul. But the emphases may differ as the arts of prudence are applied to sometimes dramatically different circumstances.

Napoleon: Greatness without Moderation

De Gaulle famously remarked in *The Edge of the Sword*, his 1932 book on military and political leadership, that no statesman worth his salt is inspired by a vision of "evangelical perfection." The Sermon on the Mount cannot provide practical guidance for a statesman imbued with a sense of personal and political honor and committed to the defense of one's homeland and the civilized patrimony of the West. And yet de Gaulle never considered power politics, military expansion, or personal ambition to be ends in themselves. As his treatment of Napoleon Bonaparte in the central chapter of his 1938 book, *France and Her Army*, illustrates, he faulted Napoleon for failing to appreciate the very serious limits of military glory. Napoleon's prodigious military and political successes undermined his capacity to acknowledge limits, and as a result, his political plans for the French domination of Europe "increasingly lost all touch with reality." After the peace of Tilsit in 1807, he bled the French dry and pursued a path that left her "crushed, invaded, drained of blood and courage, smaller than when he had taken control of her destinies, condemned to ill-drawn frontiers." De Gaulle, like Chateaubriand before him, was enough of a romantic to be genuinely awed by Napoleon's prodigious career and superhuman military virtues. But in the end, de Gaulle's outlook was rather more classical than romantic; his admiration for Napoleon did not get in the way of his final judgment that Napoleon's contempt for limits and restraints finally led "outraged reason" to exact "her inexorable vengeance."

Students of de Gaulle's thought and action such as myself and the French historian Patrice Gueniffey have stressed his self-conscious efforts, indebted to both classical and Christian thought and sensibilities, to avoid any disassociation of grandeur and "measure" at the theoretical or practical levels. As Gueniffey helpfully points out in his splendid recent book *Napoleon and De Gaulle: Heroes and History*, de Gaulle was a patriot and nationalist whose fidelity to France was "tempered by liberal and Christian values." And the Gaullist vision of "greatness of soul," the so-called man of character, explicitly repudiated what he contemptuously called in his 1946 Bayeux address "the adventure of dictatorship." That false path necessarily culminated, de Gaulle thought, in "disaster and bloodshed," destroying civilized liberty along the way. The path of Napoleon, with its unilateral emphasis on military glory and power politics and its contempt for limits and law, was definitely not de Gaulle's way. De Gaulle could not imagine true political greatness without the exercise of the cardinal virtues at the service of a broader fidelity to country, faith, and civilization even as he acknowledged the role of deception in statecraft too. De Gaulle was a modern statesman-thinker with the soul of a classic. He believed that true courage was at the service of ends and purposes that far transcended personal ambition shorn of genuine nobility.

Classical Honor Meets Christian Humility

De Gaulle was also a Catholic whose soul fruitfully oscillated between the requirements of classical honor and Christian fidelity to restraints and limits, finding that space characterized by the elevating moral obligations inherent in civilization as such. For his part, Churchill admired Christianity from afar, combining the Ciceronian virtues with a genuine respect for liberal and Christian civilization. He will always be remembered as the indomitable leader whose eloquent and spirited rhetoric gave the English every reason to resist the future offered by Nazi despotism: "the abyss of a new Dark Age, made more sinister, and perhaps more protracted, by the lights of perverted science," as he said in his Finest Hour Speech of June 18, 1940. Churchill was the indefatigable enemy of appeasement, the noble statesman who saw that pusillanimity before Hitler's soulless pagan barbarism would only bring dishonor and defeat to an old, proud, and free people and would risk the survival of civilization itself. Churchill knew, as Cicero, Washington, Burke, and de Gaulle also knew and appreciated, that freedom could not be sustained without a recovery of "martial health and moral vigor as in the olden time." These eloquent if seemingly archaic words are from a famous speech of October 5, 1938, lamenting Chamberlain's capitulation at Munich and the false reassurance of peace this had given the British people.

Churchill, too, was a Ciceronian who loved peace and preferred it to war, as Herodotus said all reasonable human beings should do. His love of true peace, his disdain for tyranny and the totalitarian subjugation of the soul, led him, in every fiber of his being, to resist the new and terrible world order proffered by Hitler and his minions. But it should be noted that Churchill was not a neoconservative in foreign policy *avant la lettre*. Like Burke, he knew prudential judgment must address the concrete particularity of great moments of history. Not every moment is a repetition of Munich 1938. Sometimes good sense and prudential reasoning demand restraint, especially if one is dealing with a sane regime still informed by civilized values. At the end of his political career, worried about the delicate character of the so-called nuclear balance of terror, Churchill called for a reasonable accommodation between the Western democracies and the post-Stalin leadership of the Soviet Union. We know from his Iron Curtain Speech of March 5, 1946, that Churchill, a lifelong anti-Bolshevik, wanted to address the Soviet Union from a position of strength. He truly lamented the loss of liberties in the great nations and states of East-Central Europe for whom he had the deepest respect and affection. But Churchill, too, finally preferred the "urbane virtues" to the "martial ones." And the specter of nuclear annihilation made the necessity of a broader "European settlement" even more urgent in his mind. But because he was a friend of peace, he was willing to make war where principle and prudence and genuine honor demanded.

Classical Honor and the Sermon on the Mount

A brief excursus on the closing paragraphs of Chapter 17 of *The Gathering Storm*, "The Tragedy of Munich," will serve to highlight the moderation and good sense that underlay Churchill's spirited resistance to Nazi tyranny and imperialism and to misplaced efforts to appease a malignant regime whose ambitions knew no limits. In the spirit of Cicero, Churchill fully acknowledges that "meekness and humility" rather than underlying bellicosity often point toward mutual understanding and accommodation between human beings and nations. Wars, Churchill says, have often been needlessly precipitated by "firebrands." "How many misunderstandings which led to wars could have been removed by temporizing! How often countries fought cruel wars and then after a few years of peace found themselves not only friends but allies." In most cases, Churchill recommends the path of restraint, of accommodation and self-limitation. But, like Charles de Gaulle,

Churchill rejects the applicability of the Sermon on the Mount ("the last word in Christian ethics") to the conduct of statesmen in foreign affairs. Churchill is wrong to think that Christ was speaking politically in the Sermon on the Mount or in any way recommending pacifism to those in positions of political responsibility. There is no evidence that the Prince of Peace espoused pacifism in politics or was providing anything other than the demanding requirements of discipleship from a radically perfectionist or eschatological point of view. Still, Churchill is not wrong that there are enduring and abiding tensions between classical honor, which he esteems and endorses, and Christian ethics understood as beneficent mercy and at times great forbearance in the face of evil.

The path of honor that Churchill ends up recognizing would entail fidelity to democratic Czechoslovakia, an ally of France (and indirectly of Britain), as she was threatened by the totalitarian wolf that was Nazi Germany. In truth, the mixture of fidelity, forbearance, goodwill, classical honor, and moral realism advocated by Churchill, and at the heart of his thought and action during the dangerous years of the 1930s, was informed by both Ciceronian greatness of soul and a love of peace. The former melds together greatness and moderation; the latter, peace, resists pacifism and in Churchill's case owes much to Christian chivalry and the traditions of the English (and European) gentleman. Modern ideological abstractions such as power and power politics, Machiavellian (pseudo-) realism, and charismatic leadership, not to mention facile confusions of authority with domination (something common to the *Machtpolitiker* Max Weber and the nihilist antinomian Michel Foucault), played no role in shaping Churchill's thought and action. A fuller examination of the statecraft and political reflection of such divergent yet altogether noble statesmen as Edmund Burke, George Washington,

Abraham Lincoln, and Václav Havel would establish the same point: the reductive and cynical philosophy of power, pleasure, and charisma can say nothing of substance about the thought, virtues, motives, and public spiritedness that inform the noble statesman who self-consciously attempts to conjugate thought and action, greatness and moderation, while eschewing power and pleasure as ends in themselves. Classical and Christian political philosophy can make sense of the statesman as thinker, of magnanimity informed by an appreciation of limits and self-restraint; modern political philosophy and modern social science can only explain away such statesmen.

Magnanimity and Restraint

Book I of Cicero's *On Duties*, influential in Western education for a millennium or more, provides the most satisfying account, at once descriptive and normative, of the self-understanding and the moral and intellectual virtues of the statesman-thinker as the great tradition conceived him. Cicero imagined a virtuous statesman "who anticipated future events by reflection," thus embodying the foresight at the heart of the Latin concept of *prudentia*. "A spirit great and lofty," as Cicero puts it in a strikingly high-minded formulation, respects the inheritance of the past, cultivates the city in which he finds himself, and prudently anticipates the challenges and dangers that are likely to arise in the future. Such a statesman attempts to avoid rash and unnecessary military conflicts but will fight to the death if "slavery and disgrace" are at stake. Cicero's model of the great-souled spirit meets Christianity halfway (avant la lettre, to be sure), spiritualizing magnanimity and emphasizing humility and restraint as much as or more than self-assertion or precipitous adventures. But the noble statesman will never accommodate himself to peace at any price or the indignity of true tyranny or civic slavery.

Solon: The Statesman as Mediator

The true, noble statesman according to Cicero follows Plato in seeing the governing of the commonwealth as guardianship; he is in some deep spiritual sense "oblivious to [his] own advantage," at least in any vulgar sense of the term. Above all, he hates civic discord and dissension and aims to be just to the legitimate claims of the rich and the poor, the few and the many. Sedition and discord, culminating in civil war, are the great evils to be avoided. Like Solon's statesmanship described and lauded by Aristotle in *The Constitution of Athens*, he neither keeps the many in chains nor allows the "best," the upper class, to oppress the people as a whole. As Solon put it in his own striking political poetry, recounted by Aristotle:

> I gave to the mass of people such rank as befitted their need,
> I took not away their honor, and I granted not their greed;
> While those who were rich in power, who in wealth were
> glorious and great,
> I bethought me that naught should befall them unworthy their
> splendor and state;
> So I stood with my shield out-stretched, and both were safe in
> its sight,
> And I would not that either should triumph, when the triumph
> was not with right.

Solon is perhaps the model par excellence of the Aristotelian and Ciceronian statesman as a just and honorable mediator between the enduring political distinctions. He was famously of middle-class background himself, a point both Aristotle and Cicero stress. Like Solon, Cicero defended the inviolability of private property against rapacious oligarchs, thieving tyrants, and men of "unbalanced soul," to quote Solon once again. But Cicero's was, in the end, not an "oligarchic" defense of property; he welcomed new property and social advancement on the part of "new men" such as himself as well as industrious and law-abiding plebeians. When Churchill opposed socialism in Britain after 1945, criticizing "the gospel of envy" and ignorance of the true sources of prosperity and productivity, he did it in the name of a social vision he called "property-owning democracy." He wanted tenants to become owners and thus true citizens with a stake in the social order. In contrast, the socialists, he believed, "want everyone to be the tenants of the State." Once again, Churchill's humane conservative vision was very much in the tradition of the classical statesmanship defended and embodied by Cicero and Solon.

Final Lessons

The political philosopher Leo Strauss, who knew something about both philosophy and tyranny, profoundly admired Churchill, whom he saw as a "magnanimous statesman" defending the cause of civilization in the twentieth century against the "insane tyrant" Hitler. Paying tribute to Churchill before his students in a class on political philosophy upon hearing of his death on January 25, 1965, Strauss suggested that those who study politics have no higher task, "no higher duty," "than to remind ourselves and our students of political greatness, human greatness, of the peaks of human excellence," in contrast to even "brilliant" mediocrity. To study politics accurately, realistically, and scientifically is to appreciate how things come to sight to thoughtful and morally serious human beings and citizens.

And Strauss no doubt would appreciate the profound observation of the Russian writer and Nobel laureate Aleksandr Solzhenitsyn, who, inspired by the noble if thwarted efforts of the great early twentieth-century Russian statesman Pyotr Stolypin to save prerevolutionary Russia from both reactionary petrification and revolutionary nihilism and tyranny, incisively remarked in *November 1916*: "Nothing is more difficult than drawing a middle line for social development. The loud mouth, the big fist, the bomb, the prison bars are of no help to you, as they are to those at the two extremes. Following the middle path demands the utmost self-control, the most inflexible courage, the most precise knowledge." Such statesmanship demands self-command in the highest sense of the term.

The moderation that Cicero, Strauss, and Solzhenitsyn invoke in their different ways has nothing to do with slow-motion accommodation to cultural rot or moral nihilism or doctrinaire egalitarianism. It is instead an enduring if embattled form of human excellence worthy of our continuing admiration. It demands that all the powers of the soul and the full range of the intellectual and moral virtues be utilized at the service of "commanding practical reason" and of civilization itself. This model of reflective statesmanship, judiciously melding thought and action, greatness and moderation, and humble deference to the divine and moral law, rivals contemplative philosophy as an enduring peak of human excellence. To recover the lost art of statesmanship, we must free ourselves from dogmatic, cynical, and reductive categories that block our access to things as they are.

Sources and Suggested Readings

For an incisive account of (commanding) practical reason and its relationship to natural law, see Pierre Manent, *Natural Law and*

Human Rights: Toward a Recovery of Practical Reason, translated by Ralph C. Hancock, foreword by Daniel J. Mahoney (Notre Dame, IN: University of Notre Dame Press, 2020).

The roots of modern "realism" and the reduction of politics and the whole of human life to "power" and power relations can be found in such works as Machiavelli's *The Prince*, Hobbes's *Leviathan*, and with a characteristic Germanic extremism in the later writings of Friedrich Nietzsche and (to a lesser extent) Max Weber. A rather domesticated version informs contemporary international relations theory.

I am indebted to Raymond Aron's lucid recovery of civic and moral common sense in Aron, *Democracy and Totalitarianism*, translated by Valence Ionescu (New York: Frederick A. Praeger Publishers, 1969). The original edition was published in French in 1965. The quotes are drawn from pages 23 and 24.

My thoughts and reflections on Cicero are indebted in particular to the writings of Pierre Manent and Gregory Bruce Smith. Both approach him phenomenologically and see the great Roman statesman–political philosopher as a bridge between ancient and modern theory and practice. I have used Benjamin Patrick Newton's extremely accurate and accessible translation of Cicero's *On Duties* published in the Agora series of Cornell University Press in 2016. For Cicero's critique of philosophical and political hedonism, see Book I, section 5, and Book III, sections 116–20. All remaining quotations are drawn from *On Duties*, Book I, sections 71–92. This section of *On Duties* is a veritable tractate on political nobility and magnanimous statesmanship informed by the cardinal virtues and a sense of decency, high-mindedness, and restraint.

For Mary Ann Glendon's excellent account of Cicero's melding of political nobility and eros of the mind, see Glendon, *The Forum*

and the Tower (New York: Oxford University Press, 2011), especially pages 24–25.

For de Gaulle's searching account of Napoleon's willful separation of grandeur and moderation, see Charles de Gaulle, *France
and Her Army*, translated by F. L. Dash (London: Hutchinson &
Company, 1944). The quotes are drawn from pages 45, 54–55, and
60. For the broader sources of de Gaulle's melding of grandeur and
moderation, see Patrice Gueniffey, *Napoleon and de Gaulle: Heroes
and History*, translated by Steven Rendall (Cambridge, MA: The
Belknap Press of Harvard University Press, 2020), 221–23.

Churchill's magisterial reflection on the Sermon on the Mount,
ethics, and honor can be found in Winston S. Churchill, *The Second World War, Volume 1: The Gathering Storm* (Boston, MA:
Houghton Mifflin Company, 1948), 287–88.

For Aristotle's superb account of Solon's noble mediation between
the rich and the poor, the few and the many, see *Constitution of Athens*, sections 5–13. I have used F. G. Kenyon's translation published by
Oxford University Press in 1920. The moving and instructive excerpt
from Solon's political poetry is drawn from section 12.

Churchill's defense of "property-owning democracy" is best
articulated in a speech on May 28, 1948, in Perth, Scotland ("Social-
ism Is the Philosophy of Failure"). It can be found in Winston S.
Churchill, *Never Give In!: Winston Churchill's Speeches* (London:
Bloomsbury Academic, 2013), 372–73, edited by his grandson
Winston S. Churchill.

Leo Strauss's noble articulation of Churchill's greatness is
reproduced as an opening epigraph in Harry V. Jaffa, ed., *Statesmanship: Essays in Honor of Sir Winston Spencer Churchill* (Durham,
NC: Carolina Academic Press, 1981). Strauss's brief but penetrating eulogy of Churchill provides a particularly insightful account
of true political science.

Solzhenitsyn's beautiful evocation of the soul of the statesman pursuing the "middle path" can be found in *November 1916: The Red Wheel / Knot II*, translated from the Russian by H. T. Willetts (New York: Farrar, Straus and Giroux, 1999), 59. Solzhenitsyn contrasts Stolypin's tough-minded moderation with the "false liberalism" of those such as the Russian Kadets who turned a blind eye to revolutionary terrorism and to all forms of leftist extremism more broadly.

Greatness, resolve, a wish for the public's esteem, but governed by duty, by public duty in particular, and by a height of soul that would not stoop. So Washington's "magnanimity" appeared to his protégé [John] Marshall and to others, Jeffersonian as well as Federalist, who knew the man at first hand. Washington seems to have been great as well as good, and good as well as great. Whereas Xenophon's Cyrus turns justice, honor, and duty into instruments of imperial ambition, Washington's ambition served justice, honor, and duty. Whereas Thucydides' Alcibiades ranges beyond his country's laws and limits toward glorious victories and empire, Washington defended his democratic republic, accepted its limitations, and framed and settled its fundamental laws. Napoleon, an authority on imperial ambition, is supposed to have lamented on Elba: "They wanted me to be another Washington."

The combination of such goodness with such greatness is hard to understand.

—ROBERT FAULKNER,
The Case for Greatness: Honorable Ambition and Its Critics

2

THE GREAT AND THE GOOD: CLASSICAL POLITICAL PHILOSOPHY AND HONORABLE AMBITION

Rarely today does one come across a book of political philosophy that freshly illuminates the nature of reality as well as the great questions informing the Western tradition of political reflection. In the face of too much abstract theorizing, the phenomena of moral and political life in all their complexity and amplitude are obscured. But there are rare if notable exceptions. In *The Case for Greatness: Honorable Ambition and the Critics* (Yale University Press, 2007)[1], the Boston College political theorist Robert Faulkner wrote that rare book that helps one see the world better and more deeply. His book remains a summa of learning, reflection, and wisdom, the product of a truly mature effort to overcome "those obscuring theories" that get in the way of an appreciation of "honorable or statesmanlike ambition" (*CG*, 1,11,12). In the course of this chapter, I hope to make clear my considerable debts to and my reservations about Faulkner's admirable approach to the study of honorable ambition.

---

1 All references to this work will henceforth be cited in the body of the text parenthetically as *CG* followed by the appropriate page number.

Faulkner's starting point is the "big divide" between, on the one hand, "thoughtful citizens" and "appreciative historians" who still acknowledge those great statesmen whose qualities of soul are indispensable for "defending, reforming, and founding a free country" (*CG*, 1), and, on the other hand, the various theorists who have succumbed to skepticism, cynicism, and doctrinaire egalitarianism regarding the great and the good. Today, of course, one would need to make reference to a new nihilism and a new and aggressive iconoclasm that strikes out at nearly all the great statesmen of the past as racists and exemplars of "white supremacy." But this reflects madness—"metaphysical madness," as Edmund Burke famously called it—fevered ideology, far more than mere cynicism or skepticism. In the tradition of Leo Strauss, Faulkner establishes that the common-sense distinctions between honorable ambition, timeserving mediocrity, and the truly rapacious kind of ambition shorn of "justice, love, nobility, and friendship" (*CG*, 8) are essential to any reasonable comprehension of human affairs. Drawing on Plato's, Xenophon's, and Aristotle's insights into ambition and its limits, Faulkner recovers the fundamental and enduring difference between the ambition of a noble statesman such as Lincoln who aimed to be worthy of the esteem of his fellow citizens and the imperial ambition of a Cyrus the Great or Napoleon, not shorn of a certain greatness, which gradually became indistinguishable from "cold despotism" (*CG*, 9).

In a particularly impressive chapter on Xenophon's *Education of Cyrus*, Faulkner demonstrates how Cyrus the Great's seemingly flawless quest for imperial grandeur was ultimately deformed by "imperial hollowness" (*CG*, 127). Xenophon's remarkably "engaging work" turns out to be less simple and less "adoring" than it might appear at first glance. To be sure, Cyrus gains an empire "with a minimum of oppression and killing and a maximum of benefiting and cleverness." Yet for Xenophon, Cyrus's "instrumental rationality is not enough" since Cyrus is completely bereft of the Socratic virtues Xenophon so admired (on that admiration, see in particular Book 1 of the *Memorabilia*). As Faulkner states so well, "In *The Education of Cyrus*, Cyrus's desire for superiority edges aside justice, love, nobility, and friendship as well as deep thoughtfulness—all" (*CG*, 8–9). Cyrus's imperial grandeur "is an activity without a serious end, and it is renown in the opinion of those he disdains and enervates" (*CG*, 176). In the end, Cyrus is a desiccated human being, a soulless despot. He is a model more for Machiavelli than for the quasi-Socratic Xenophon.

As a result, the heart and soul of Faulkner's defense of "honorable ambition" is an explication of the Aristotelian notion of *megalopsychia*, magnanimity or "greatness of soul."[2] Faulkner rightly insists that Aristotle's portrait of magnanimity is the *locus classicus* of all efforts to do justice to the mixture of "greatness and goodness" that defines true statesmanship. Aristotle is the "philosophical portraitist" (*CG*, 18) par excellence of the gentleman-statesman, the first and still unsurpassed "philosopher of the inside of a gentleman" (*CG*, 17). His is both description *and* defense of magnanimity but one that brings to light the tensions and complications inherent in the soul of that rare human being who "thinks himself worthy of great things—and is indeed worthy of them."

The second chapter of Faulkner's book consists of a fascinating forty-page explication of the single chapter in *The Nicomachean Ethics* (Book 4, Chapter 3) that attempts to come to terms with magnanimity, "the crown of the virtues" (*NE*, 1124a1–4). Faulkner supplements his careful and suggestive reading of this

---

2 I have followed Faulkner's own translation of the text rather than any of the well-known available translations of the *Nicomachean Ethics*. See more on this issue in the "Sources and Suggested Readings" that closes out this chapter.

foundational chapter with discussions of other parts of the *Ethics* and *Politics* of Aristotle that round out the political philosopher's account of the public-spirited gentleman-statesman. The "great-souled" man that Aristotle was the first to theorize comes to sight not as a "charismatic leader" or fame seeker in the modern style made famous by Max Weber, wooing the masses with an invisible charism accompanied by vivid displays and spectacles. Rather he is a man of "noble and good character" (*NE,* 1124a3–4). As Aristotle's (and Faulkner's) chapter unfolds, the complications build, and the virtue of magnanimity is revealed to be riddled with tensions. But Aristotle never withdraws his initial claim that the magnanimous man is both great and good, even if qualifications—and reservations, even corrections—become subtly apparent.

In Aristotle's account, the great-souled man legitimately claims great honors for himself. His pride is neither sin nor arrogant usurpation. At the same time, he "holds himself moderately" toward "good and bad fortune" (*NE,* 1124a14–15). He desires recognition for his superiority but only from those who are morally serious (what Aristotle calls the *spoudaios*), whose opinion really counts. Faulkner ably captures the great-souled man's reticence regarding honor itself: "His is superiority from the heights of inner independence. He has bigger fish to fry than his own glory" (*CG,* 33). Yet as Faulkner shows, the rich Aristotelian portrait of "greatness of soul" contains its share of shadows. The magnanimous man is "unable to live in dependence on another" and only remembers the good he has done for others and not "the benefits that have been conferred" upon him (*NE,* 1124b13–14). More troublingly, he is not inclined toward admiration since "in his eyes nothing is great" (*NE,* 1125b14–15). This seems both unjust and ungenerous and bereft of true self-knowledge. He does not even pursue a life of public service in any recognizable sense: "he is hesitant and slow to act except where there is great honor or significant result at stake" (*NE*, 1124b25). Aristotle underscores that he "puts no great weight on anything" (*NE*, 1125a3–4). He appears to aspire to godlike self-sufficiency and at the end of the chapter is said to move slowly and to speak with a deep voice. At one point, he is compared to the capricious Zeus (*NE*, 1124b17–18), which in this context is perhaps more a criticism than a compliment.

Faulkner is fully aware of these complications. He lays them out with a rare and admirable dialectical subtlety. He shows how the desire of the great-souled man for self-sufficiency needs to be corrected by the later emphasis on justice and the common good in the *Ethics* as well as, in the *Politics*, an ample defense of rule of law, patriotism, public spiritedness, and a "mixed regime" that takes into account the good of the popular elements in any political community.[3] More fundamentally, Aristotle reveals the limits of all moral virtue shorn of the self-knowledge made possible by philosophical reflection. But Faulkner rightly insists that Aristotle's ultimate subordination of magnanimity to philosophy entails a "clarifying and purifying of practical virtue, not an obliteration or replacement of it" (*CG*, 55). Aristotle thus avoids Plato's theoretical extremism, his tendency to view nonphilosophical ways

---

3 Faulkner places particular emphasis on the treatment of justice in Book 5 of the *Nicomachean Ethics*, on Aristotle's "political defense of the middle class" (*CG*, 52) in Book 4 of the *Politics,* and on Aristotle's turn to an elevating liberal education in Books 7 and 8 of the same work (*CG*, 55-57). Faulkner eloquently and laconically summarizes Aristotle's intention in these sections of the *Ethics* and the *Politics*: "Greatness of soul is to defer *somewhat* (my italics) to greatness of mind, and that taste and tact helps keep the great-souled man limited in his ambition, for himself and for his country" (*CG*, 55). Aristotle moderates the autarchy or self-sufficiency of the great-souled man by tying his greatness to the common good of a free and civilized polity and to a deeper thoughtfulness about the ends and purposes of human life. In my view, this "correction" becomes more explicit, more tied to the description of the phenomenon itself, in Cicero's more ample and many-sided description of "greatness of spirit" in Book 1 of *On Duties*.

of life, however seemingly noble, as intrinsically inferior or even mutilated in comparison to the true virtue of the philosopher.

Still, in my opinion, Faulkner goes too far in simply identifying the great-souled man with the public-spirited gentleman-states-man. The philanthropy of the "great-souled man" is qualified by his refusal to acknowledge his debts to others, and his quest for self-sufficiency is ultimately in deep tension with a generous appre-ciation of moral limits and what one owes one's country. Instead of resting content with this ambiguity, Faulkner finally reads the great-souled man (in light of Aristotle's subsequent "correction") as a public-spirited statesman, one who combines greatness, good-ness, and patriotism in ways that are genuinely admirable.

Faulkner can do so only by conflating later exemplars of "hon-orable ambition" such as Washington, Lincoln, and Churchill with Aristotle's canonical account of "greatness of soul." Through-out the text, Faulkner gives examples from the life and writings of such modern exemplars of magnanimity to illustrate Aristotle's understanding of greatness of soul and does so very effectively. He is not wrong to attribute self-conscious magnanimity to some of the greatest democratic statesmen of modern times. Despite our official claims to the contrary, free communities finally depend upon the art of statesmanship to found, reform, and defend regimes of liberty.

Whether it is a matter of Lincoln's defense of his fellow dem-ocratic citizens against those tyrannical souls who belong to the "tribe of the lion and the eagle" (to cite his 1838 Lyceum Address) or Churchill's eloquent appeals to personal and political honor in the struggle against modern totalitarianism or Washington's embodiment of statesmanlike honor and dignity in a way that reminded his contemporaries of Roman *gravitas* and *dignitas*, the modern world has indeed witnessed rare, admirable, and noble displays of human and political excellence. And let our contemporary iconoclasts remember that Washington freed his slaves and provided for their education and economic provision in his final will and testament. But these distinctively modern manifestations of "greatness of soul" bring together aristocratic and democratic virtues in ways that depart from the letter and spirit of Aristotelian magnanimity (even as they build on Aristotle's wise and humane philosophical correction of the "autarky" inherent in the deepest longings of the magnanimous man). An instructive example provided by Faulkner helps illustrate the need to differentiate magnanimity proper (and its rare and admirable modern manifestations) from the "complicated" and more problematic Aristotelian description.

In an excellent chapter, "Obscuring the Truly Great: Washington and Modern Theories of Fame," Faulkner discusses various interpretations of the "iconic American gentleman-statesman," George Washington (*CG*, 177–97). He contrasts the historian Douglas Adair's account of the American founder's motives with that provided by John Marshall, one of Washington's earliest as well as best biographers. Adair drew on a complicated "republican tradition," largely of scholarly construction, that was said to incorporate Plutarch, Machiavelli, and the Enlightenment philosopher-statesman Francis Bacon (*CG*, 178). In Adair's presentation, this tradition helps us understand that fame, the quest for this worldly glory, lay behind the public spiritedness of a man such as Washington. In contrast, in his *Life of Washington*, Marshall, a statesman of great distinction himself, drew on Cicero's account of the priority of duty in *De Officiis* (*On Duties*) to account for Washington's mixture of gravitas, high character, public spirit, and dedication to the cause of liberty (*CG*, 187–90). Marshall, like his friend and inspiration Washington, was unquestionably dedicated to the *modern* cause of constitutionalism, representative government, and the rights of man. But when describing Washington's virtues, Marshall did not hesitate to turn to a *classical* account of public duty and virtue. I am speaking not of Aristotle's original description of magnanimity but rather of Cicero's modified and—dare I say—improved account of that virtue. As Faulkner himself shows, Cicero's version of magnanimity "dwells on the honorable duties involved in free public life" (*CG*, 187). Its twin focus is on "Stoic dutifulness and free politics" (*CG*, 188). Cicero deprecates the apolitical hedonism of the Epicurean philosophical tradition and defends the virtues that flourish in free political communities.[4] Duty, a concern for justice and for one's fellow men and citizens, and a preference for free and dignified political life become the defining traits of the public-spirited gentleman-statesman. Faulk-

4 Cicero forthrightly defended the arts of high moral and political prudence against the debased and corrupting Epicurean view that prudence was no more than an instrument for "furnishing pleasures and repelling pains" (*On Duties*, 3, 118). And the first twelve sections of Book 1 of his *On the Republic* begin with a robust defense of those who put their virtues at the service of the commonwealth, among whom he counts himself for achieving "simultaneously something memorable in managing the republic and a certain ability to expound the meaning (*ratio*) of political things" (*On the Republic*, 1, 13). Cicero locates his own considerable authority as a guide to political things in both his "experience" as a statesman and his "eagerness for learning and teaching" that was inseparable from being a philosopher (*On the Republic*, 1, 13). Cicero opposed the growing tyrannical ambitions of Caesar and the even more base tyrannical aspirations of Marc Antony in the name of free politics, civic duty, and moral virtue. He even argued that tyrannicide was for true Romans a noble deed, in fact "the most beautiful of all superb deeds" (*On Duty*, 3,19). As a statesman, Cicero was not without flaws: Plutarch criticizes his rhetoric for combining noble eloquence at the service of the republic with vanity and excessive self-praise. But Plutarch ends on a note of admiration: as a Roman consul and political man confronting Cataline and his accomplices, Cicero verified Plato's great prediction that "every political community will be delivered from its calamities, when, by the favor of fortune, great power unites with justice in one person." This is high praise indeed. And Plutarch adds that Cicero was always generous in acknowledging true greatness in others. In this important sense, Cicero lived up to his own model of "the greatness of spirit," the generous magnanimity, that informs authentic statesmanship.

ner nicely captures the intention of Cicero's *On Duties*: this admirable book "educates free citizens to look up to philosophers and not to disdain them or kill them. But its principal task is to foster the justice and noble spirit needed for free politics, which requires simplification and moralization of instruction as well as a salutary philosophy" (*CG*, 190). But there is much truth in this salutary simplification since moral virtue and free politics crucially depend upon each other and have an integrity all their own. Cicero thus makes classical political philosophy and free, republican politics crucial allies in the effort to sustain civilized existence against both tyranny and barbarism.

In any case, this much has become clear: Washington embodied magnanimity as it had been modified by several post-Aristotelian sources. These included Cicero's republican appropriation of a qualified Stoicism, a Christian emphasis on common humanity, and the modern doctrine of the rights of man. Lincoln, too, was unarguably a modern exemplar of magnanimity, but his abhorrence of slavery and his defense of human equality owed much to biblical religion and its profound anthropological truth. Churchill was largely "pagan" in his moral and philosophical bearing, as the historian John Lukacs has provocatively argued. But as Churchill himself put it in *Thoughts and Adventures*, in a passage highlighted by Faulkner, the English statesman knew that "the moral philosophy and the spiritual conceptions of men and nations" that were critical for the defense of the dignity of man in an age beset by what Faulkner himself called "new ideological tyrannies and new scientific and industrial powers of destruction" (quoted in *CG*, 4–5) owed a great deal to Christian ethics. Whatever his personal religious convictions, Churchill's capacious soul itself was unthinkable outside the context of the Christian West, of a civilization shaped by the humanizing tension between Athens and Jerusalem, magnanimity and humility. In that sense, he was a partisan of Christian ethics as well as an exemplar of classical magnanimity.

Faulkner's admirable defense of a tradition of thought and action that "took seriously what is good and true as well as what is strong and great" would be even more persuasive if he had reflected more systematically on the Roman, Christian, and broadly democratic contributions to and modifications of what I am tempted to call a tradition of magnanimity. As I have suggested, that tradition incorporated and developed Aristotle's restrained but fundamental critique of magnanimity by weaving together pride and self-restraint, the desire for prominence with public duty. This tradition moderated magnanimity while acknowledging its just and elevating claims.

One of the strengths of Robert Faulkner's elegant book (it contains no shortage of quotable aphorisms) is the way it turns genealogy against those who see in it the preferred instrument for debunking what is seemingly worthy of respect and admiration. In this reductive modern tradition, to turn to the origin of things is by definition to expose the groundlessness of that which is presupposed to have feet of clay. Faulkner stands this tradition on its head. By returning to the profound philosophical origins of the contemporary prejudice against "honorable Ambition," he shows that moral and political greatness remain unscathed if only we have the courage to trust what we see and experience rather than the dogmas put forward in the name of a vulgar conception of "enlightenment."

Faulkner convincingly argues that the "slashing critique" (*CG*, 10) of noble greatness of soul by Thomas Hobbes was built on one dogmatic assumption after another. Honorable ambition was reduced to mere "vainglory." Hobbes's famous "laws of reason" in *Leviathan* (1651) are no more than prescriptions for niceness or inoffensiveness, and moral judgments are nothing more than rival tastes or appetites. This is reductionism of the most transparent sort. Hobbes assaults traditional morals in a sweeping critique that is more polemic than argument. In light of Hobbes's lowering of the human horizon, Kant admirably attempted to restore the dignity of the moral life, to inform the modern "philosophy of equal rights with a new idea of righteousness" (*CG*, 228) tied to an affirmation of the universal moral law and the moral equality of men. But there is a large dose of dogmatism in Kant's insistence on "autonomy" and his reliance on historical progress and the movement of history to substitute for the political virtue of men and citizens. At the end of the modern movement with Nietzsche, a concern for noble greatness of soul "comes storming back" (*CG*, 242) in a manner that went a long way toward discrediting the idea of a "politics of greatness." This poet-philosopher-legislator expresses a "bitter contempt" for the "virtue of humanity" (*CG*, 241). He "eulogizes both Shakespeare and the 'blond beast'" (*CG*, 242) even as his thought gives way to limitless relativism. He admires human excellence in a woefully distorted form, one deeply at odds with moderation and practical reason. His is finally a path of perdition.

Against the abstractions that dominate modern philosophical thought, Faulkner calls on us to trust our own judgment and experience. As the classical historians and philosophers appreciated so well, "decent people have an eye in particular circumstances for the fitting or correct thing to do. For Aristotle, that discernment, admittedly shaped by correct dispositions, is near the core of moral judgment" (*CG*, 234). That is the mind's eye, the heart's eye, and it is a powerful form of cognitive judgment. Alas, Faulkner demonstrates that common sense will get little support from what passes for "political theory" in elite academic circles today. A contemporary political philosopher such as John Rawls succumbed to dogmatic egalitarianism and gave next to no consideration to the qualities of soul necessary to preserve a free country (*CG*, 200–210, especially 206–207). In her illuminating book *The Human Condition* (1958), Hannah Arendt spoke much more promisingly about the need to overcome the "loss of common sense" (*CG*, 218) promoted by skeptical modern philosophy. She called for the recovery of "public space," the realm of freedom that still had a place for "the glory of great deeds" (*CG*, 216). But Faulkner shows that Arendt tended to aestheticize politics, identifying "action" with the act of distinguishing oneself by "breaking with the everyday" (*CG*, 213), a thought clearly inspired by Martin Heidegger, hardly a defender of moderation or political liberty. Too often she spoke about public space as if it provided a stage for theatrical display more than a humanizing arena for moderating conflict and pursuing the civic common good (*CG*, 216). Surprisingly, she gave little or no thought to the "old absolutes" such as "prudence, wisdom, and decent character" (*CG*, 214). She is, in the end, too estranged from the cardinal virtues and too enamored of politics as "agonistic" display.

Modern "theorizing" has contributed in its own way to the extremes of tyranny and total war. One way it has done so is by providing arguments to "dictatorial transformers of civilization" such as Robespierre, Lenin, Hitler, or Che Guevara. But great democratic statesmen such as FDR, Churchill, Truman, and Reagan "led the democracies to confront and then defeat the tyrannical dictators and their empires." In *The Case for Greatness*, Robert Faulkner provides a model of political philosophizing that does justice to the palpable distinction between the statesman and the tyrant, something largely lost by a political science obsessed with undifferentiated "power" and egalitarian leveling. He wisely suggests that we should not be on guard against "the evil of greatness" in the manner recommended by egalitarian dogmatists and debunkers but rather against the dangers of "evil greatness." By reminding us of the indispensability of men "good as well as great" (*CG*, 200), Faulkner renews the tradition of classical philosophy. He puts us in touch with the world of common sense, of virtue and vice, of the noble and base, of intellectual reflection and moral self-restraint, that lies before us if we but open ourselves to it. Whatever my occasional reservations or qualifications, Faulkner's book will remain an indispensable guide to the understanding of statesmanship and the statesman's soul as well as a most welcome invitation to the recovery of true political science.

Sources and Suggested Readings

In addition to Robert Faulkner's *The Case for Greatness: Honorable Ambition and Its Critics* (Yale University Press, 2007), it is necessary to turn to the classical sources from which he draws. For an ideal combination of clarity, accuracy, and editorial direction, I recommend the translation of Aristotle's *Nicomachean Ethics* by Robert C. Bartlett and Susan D. Collins (University of Chicago Press, 2011). The best editions of Xenophon's *Memorabilia* and *The Education of Cyrus* are available in translations by Wayne Ambler and Amy L. Bonnette in the Agora Series from Cornell University Press. See the bibliographical note at the end of Chapter 1 for the recommendations for the very fine translations of Cicero's *On Duties* and *On the Republic* that also appeared in the Agora Series, founded by Allan Bloom and presently edited by Thomas L. Pangle.

I have relied on Pamela Mensch's translation of "The Life of Cicero" in *The Age of Caesar: Five Roman Lives*, translated by

Pamela Mensch, preface and notes by James Romm (Norton, 2017). For Cicero's tendency to "praise and magnify himself," see pp. 195–96; for his generosity in praising the authentic greatness of others, see p.196; and for an account of his fundamental decency and love of country, p. 224. Plutarch's great praise of Cicero's union of wisdom and justice appears in the brief "Comparison" he wrote of Cicero and the Athenian statesman and orator Demosthenes. It can be found in all the complete versions of Plutarch's *Parallel Lives*.

Hannah Arendt's *The Human Condition* (University of Chicago Press, 1958 for the original edition) is the most thoughtful and rhetorically evocative effort to return to classical greatness and to the "public space" of the Greek *polis* on essentially modernist and egalitarian grounds. This effort fails for all the reasons noted by Robert Faulkner in *The Case for Greatness*.

I do not vilify theory and speculation—no, because that would be
to vilify reason itself. Neque decipitur ratio, neque decipit unquam.
No, whenever I speak against theory, I mean always a weak,
erroneous, fallacious, unfounded, or imperfect theory; and one of
the ways of discovering that it is a false theory is by comparing it
with practice. This is the true touchstone of all theories which regard
man and the affairs of men—does it suit his nature in general—
does it suit his nature as modified by his habits?

—EDMUND BURKE,
"Speech on the Reform of the Representation of the
Commons in Parliament" (June 16, 1784)

We know, and it is our pride to know, that man is by his
constitution a religious animal; that atheism is against, not only
our reason but our instincts; and that it cannot prevail long. But
if, in the moment of riot, and in a drunken delirium from the
hot spirit drawn out of the alembic of hell, which in France is now
so furiously boiling, we should uncover our nakedness by throwing
off that Christian religion which has hitherto been our boast
and comfort, and one great source of civilization amongst us,
and among many other nations, we are apprehensive (being well
aware that the mind will not endure a void) that some uncouth,
pernicious, and degrading superstition, might take place of it.

—EDMUND BURKE,
Reflections on the Revolution in France (1790)

— 3 —

EDMUND BURKE:
NOBLE PRUDENCE IN THE
AGE OF IDEOLOGY

Edmund Burke, the eighteenth-century Anglo-Irish states-man, embodied the quintessence of political nobility and of the statesman as thinker or political philosopher. As Mary Ann Glendon has argued, he deserves a place with Cicero "in the Pantheon of those who excelled" in the two great domains of politics and philosophy, the "two most choice-worthy callings" according to Aristotle in his *Ethics* and *Politics*. It is true that Burke defended sound "prejudice," as he called it, as a precious vehicle for imparting the wisdom and experience of the ages, and he saw "prescriptive," right, long-established practice as the best claim to possession and proprietorship. For Burke, the identification of prejudice and prescription with "aggravated injustice," as he put it in his final political testament, *Letter to a Noble Lord* (1796), was an invitation to destroy all law, all tradition, all morality, all property, and all reverence toward the civilized inheritance that has been passed on to us. It is to perpetually reopen long and forgotten disputes. What the French revolutionaries and their intellectual fellow travelers stood for was innovation understood as perpetual "insurrection," a madly hubristic effort to always begin everything anew. "Ingratitude," Burke wrote in the *Letter to a Noble Lord*, was "the first of revolutionary virtues" and thus a vice of the highest order. It led inexorably to an ignoble and self-destructive obligation to revolt "against the order" in which one lives. The noble subjects of Burke's 1796 "Letter," the Duke of Bedford and the Earl of Lauderdale, embodied this blind insouciance, as Burke pointed out with biting eloquence. They were the beneficiaries of prescriptive rights par excellence going all the way back to the usurpations of Henry VIII. Yet they flirted with revolutionary ideas that would consume their inheritance and possibly their very lives. Not to worry, Burke added, the sheer solidity of English liberty would protect these two pathetic ideological dilettantes "from all the pickaxes of all the levelers of France." So much of Burke's elevating thought and noble bearing is entailed in this final testament. Even at his acerbic best, Burke exudes nobility of thought and character as well as profound insight.

Burke on Theory and Practice

Yet if Burke railed against the spirit of abstraction in politics, a false and destructive "metaphysics" when mistakenly applied to the realm of practice, and condemned "theory" and "speculation" divorced from the arts of prudence, he did not do so with anti-philosophical intent. His "star and compass" (a phrase we owe to John Locke) was prudence, or practical *reason*, "the god of this lower world," as he so memorably called it. Glendon is right when she argues that Burke's dismissive remarks about "theory," "metaphysics," and "speculation" were aimed at "abstract theory divorced from practical reason and experience," an interpretation amply supported by the opening epigraph at the beginning of this chapter. Burke was no enemy of human reason. But in any ideological project to remake society *de novo*, Burke saw the triumph of madness. Tyranny of a truly unprecedented sort was, in Burke's judgment, the inevitable outcome of ideological politics. As Daniel Ritchie has written, Burke's defense of practical reason and critique of ideological fanaticism remain "relevant to our present discontents." Our institutions and social order are not those that Burke confronted in Georgian England, Ritchie rightly notes. Far from it. But Ritchie adds that Burke's "passionate refutation of leveling ideology and totalist politics has lost little of its force with the passing of two centuries." Ritchie was writing in 1990 when one might have reasonably expected the Western world to have learned the key lessons from humanity's ill-fated experience with a form of ideological despotism, Marxist-Leninist-Stalinist-Maoist Communism that, along with the Hitlerite regime, made previous forms of tyranny seem tame in comparison. But those lessons were for the most part *not* learned. New ideological expressions of revolutionary or quasi-revolutionary ingratitude and repudiation are the order of the day. Burke's wisdom is thus needed as much as ever.

Burke's Profound Consistency of Purpose

I will not be the first to draw upon and endorse Winston Churchill's defense of Burke against the charge of inconsistency. As Churchill wrote in his magisterial 1932 essay "Consistency in Politics," "mean and petty" spirits cannot appreciate how Burke fought against "a domineering Monarch and a corrupt Court and Parliamentary system" at home as the intellectual leader of the Whig Party and yet sympathized with the just demands of the American colonists, fought imperial abuse in India, and opposed the oppression of Irish

Catholics (with whom he had deep ancestral roots[1]) while, at the same time, fighting with all his eloquence and might a "brutal mob and wicked sect" that was destroying France and unleashing war in the whole of Europe. Churchill adds, with an eloquence that matches Burke's own, that "no one can read the Burke of Liberty and the Burke of Authority without feeling that here was the same man pursuing the same ends, seeking the same ends of society and Government, and defending them from assaults, now from one extreme, now from the other." Churchill, a liberal conservative in the Burkean tradition, unsurprisingly gets to the heart of the matter. He saw in Burke a mix of principle and prudence at the highest and most honorable level. About this he was surely right.

The True Rights of Man

Burke is the greatest of modern thinkers who was at once a liberal and a conservative and even the founder, as many people have deemed him, of a distinctively conservative current within liberal

---

1 The always insightful and provocative Conor Cruise O'Brien has made this *the* key to understanding Burke *tout court*. One need not go nearly so far to appreciate that Burke remained a son of Ireland in important respects, a product of the influential Nagel family of County Cork on his mother's side (a distinguished part of Ireland's Catholic aristocracy) and a man who was faithfully married to his Catholic wife, Jane, for many decades. In his Introduction to his significant anthology of Burke's writings, *Reflections on the Revolution in France and Other Writings* (New York, London, Toronto: Everyman's Library), Jesse Norman describes the "private" Burke at the age of fifty in 1780: a "bespectacled Irishman" with red hair (when his wig was off), a Christian and "Christian latitudinarian" (truly respectful of Catholics and Protestant dissenters), an eminently "clubbable" figure who spoke to his wife with the "utmost tenderness"(Norman, pp. xii–xiii). It is an affecting portrait. Even as Burke fought Jacobinism with all his might, he worked to modify or eliminate Catholic disabilities in Ireland and to give aggrieved Irish Catholics some participation in the franchise. Burke saw their "universal exclusion" from the franchise, and thus from genuine political representation, as "a serious evil." See the "Letter to Sir Hercules Langrishe" in Norman, *op. cit.,* p. 603.

modernity. His cause was liberty in the most capacious yet ordered sense: "a manly, moral, regulated liberty" (*RRF*[2], 7), as he so eloquently put it in the opening pages of *Reflections on the Revolution in France* in 1790. Without in any way jettisoning eternal verities—the "Permanent Things," as T. S. Eliot called them—the Anglo-Irish statesman reaffirmed the classical principle of prudence where "circumstances…give in reality to every political principle its distinguishing colour and discriminating effect" (*RRF*, 7). In revolutionary France he saw less the restoration of "light and liberty" than a profound lawlessness in the guise of a fevered proclamation of the "pretended rights" (*RRF*, 7) of man.

In Burke's considered judgment, these rights were severed from "political reason" rightly understood. They were used to excuse the fulfilling of moral and civic obligations that are, always and everywhere, at the core of ordered or civilized liberty. Burke insisted that he was in no way opposed to the "*real* rights of men" (*RRF*, 50). Those rights draw on a concrete tradition of liberty rooted in law and gratitude toward the moral inheritance passed on by our forebears. In contrast, the "pretended rights" of the revolutionaries would "totally destroy" that inheritance while severing freedom from the primordial contract, the true social contract, that connects the living to the dead and to those yet to be born. In a justly famous passage in *Reflections*, Burke defines the "great primaeval contract of eternal society" as "a partnership in all science; a partnership in all art; a partnership in every virtue; and in all perfection" (*RRF*, 82). It is by no means limited to the concerns of the flesh and commodious self-preservation. It is a

2 I have consulted Frank Turner's edition of Burke's *Reflections on the Revolution in France*, published in the Rethinking the Western Tradition series by Yale University Press in 2003. All quotations from this edition of *Reflections on the Revolution in France* will be cited parenthetically in the body of the text followed by the appropriate page numbers.

genuinely *social* contract informed by deep indebtedness to those who came before us and of self-conscious obligation to those who will follow. Modern social contract theories, on the other hand— those proffered by Hobbes, Locke, and Rousseau with some variations—"dissolve" the body politic "into an unsocial, uncivil, unconnected chaos of elementary particles" (*RRF*, 19). Their principle is the principle of *dissolution*.

Conservative Reformation versus Radical 'Innovation'

Burke knew, in his memorable formulation, that "a state without the means of some change is without the means of its conservation" (*RRF*, 19 for all quotations in this paragraph). He saw in age-old English liberty an admirable capacity to unite "conservation and correction," even in extraordinary circumstances such as the Restoration of the monarchy after a tumultuous period of Civil War and Cromwellian despotism and the Glorious Revolution of 1688 when Britain momentarily found herself without a king. The ancient constitution of England was "regenerated," or so Burke believed, and necessary reforms were introduced precisely as reforms and not as radical innovations. The body politic was thus never "disbanded," never subjected to self-conscious and potentially nihilistic revolutionary assault. *Reformation* was its salutary principle.

The literary critic and man of letters George Watson perfectly captured Burke's thinking on these matters in a 1984 essay called "Burke's Conservative Revolution" that originally appeared in *Critical Quarterly*. As Watson points out, reform for Burke, or even conservative revolution, "has nothing to do with total change and a new start, since it arises out of a respect for the system that it seeks to improve." Burke put the matter most directly in his 1796 *Letter to a Noble Lord*, where he insisted that "to innovate is not to reform." That is what the fellow-traveling nobles whom Burke severely reprimands in his rhetorical tour de force cannot begin to recognize. Like literary intellectuals before and after them, they flirted with radical revolution "in the complete style of the Jacobins" and later the Bolsheviks. As Watson puts it, the true reformer has everything to fear from nihilistic revolution even as the "violent revolutionary has everything to fear from reforms intelligently conducted and seen to work."

Watson aptly refers to "Burke's reforming horror of complete revolution" and sees the same anti-totalitarian and anti-revolutionary impulses in a twentieth-century figure such as George Orwell. The same could be said of the Russian writer Aleksandr Solzhenitsyn, who admired the great reformer Pyotr Stolypin but despised the murderous destructiveness of Lenin and his Bolshevik minions. Reform, an essentially conserving act for Burke, presupposes the continuity of civilization. Radical innovation, in contrast, prefers destruction to the patient and arduous work of conservative reformation. Burke's great writings from the 1790s, beginning with *Reflections*, aim to inculcate precisely such an understanding and distinction. This was a central aim of his mission as statesman and political philosopher. Burke eschews both reaction and revolution for the noble path of conservative reformation.

The Old Regime: A Despotism in Appearance, Not Reality

Moreover, Burke did not believe that the "dreadful things" associated with the French Revolution even at the beginning—lawlessness, violence, mob rule, anti-religious persecution, a desecration of the most sacred symbols of the old order—were in the slightest respects "necessary." One never arrives at the "quiet shore of a tranquil and prosperous liberty" by "wad(ing) through blood and tumult." Burke had no illusions about the imperfections of the French Old Regime when revolution broke out in the spring and summer of 1789; France was, in his words, "the best of the unqualified or ill-qualified monarchies" yet "was still full of abuses" (*RRF*, 105–08 for all remaining quotations in this paragraph). While acknowledging its vices, he could not deny the right of such an order to continue in existence. He did not believe the old French monarchy "incapable or undeserving of reform." He believed that it was pure madness—"metaphysical madness," as he liked to say—that "the whole fabric" of state and society should be at once pulled down to make room "for the erection of a theoretic, experimental edifice in its place." That was the path of national suicide and self-destruction. The reign of Louis XVI, he wrote, should not be confused with "Persia bleeding under the ferocious sword of Tahmas Kouli Khân." France at the end of the old regime was, in Burke's suggestive words, "a despotism rather in appearance than in reality." Under the guise of "pure democracy" and the unadulterated rights of man, the revolutionaries were in the process of creating "a mischievous and ignoble oligarchy" with many of the features of an outright, if unprecedented, tyranny. This was no accident, according to Burke. "Absolute democracy, no more than absolute monarchy, is to be reckoned among the legitimate forms of government." Burke then draws on the authority of one of his great inspirations, Aristotle: "If I recollect rightly, Aristotle observes, that a democracy has many striking points of resemblance with a tyranny." Burke is by no means a blind, romantic partisan of the French or European Old Regime. But he remained a thoughtful advocate of conservative reform, even conservative revolution as in the American case, but never of radical innovation in the name of abstract and theoretical dogmas. In them, he saw the roots of new and truly destructive despotisms. Burke's impassioned but thoughtful critique of the French Revolution (in all its permutations) is rooted in a deep and measured commitment to ordered liberty and the continuity of Western civilization.

"Armed Doctrine" at the Service of Frenzied Atheism

At the heart of ordered liberty and our civilized inheritance, Burke saw a central place for religion, property, and an ethic of chivalry, gentlemanliness, and manners and morals that combined personal honor and moral self-restraint. Burke's liberalism was essentially conservative while presupposing all the goods and benefits of liberty under law. In his *First Letter on a Regicide Peace,* published in 1796, a year before his death, he made clear that England was not simply at war with a rival nation-state—this was "a war of a peculiar nature." Five years earlier in *Thoughts on French Affairs*, Burke had argued that the French revolutionaries were adherents of a militant secular religion as fanatical as the most fevered or fanatical religious sect. Theirs was not a political revolution in the ordinary sense but rather "a Revolution of doctrine and theoretick dogma," or as we would say today, an *ideological revolution*. The "spirit of proselytism," of fevered missionary and evangelical zeal, was central to a revolution with militantly universalist and transformative pretensions. The French Revolution was a "Colossus" with one foot abroad—with myriad admirers and fellow-travelers in England and all other European countries (and one might add, the emerging United States too). It posed a grave and immediate threat to English liberty, to the European Old Regime, to the continuity of Western civilization, and to the basic freedoms of the French people that were honored even by the kings of old.

At the heart of this new "theoretick dogma," this unappeasable "armed doctrine," Burke saw an aggressively politicized atheism with roots in a "literary cabal" (the French *philosophes* and encyclopedists) who had devised "a regular plan for the destruction of the Christian religion" (all quotations in this paragraph are drawn from *RRF*, 94). In a memorable passage from *Reflections*, Burke adds that "this object they pursued with a degree of zeal which hitherto had been discovered only in the propagators of some system of piety." This cabal, which is by no means a figment of Burke's counterrevolutionary imagination, combined fanaticism with real prominence in literature, the sciences, and the arts. Like the Russian *intelligents* of the late nineteenth century, they mocked and targeted everyone who remained committed to traditional "morals and true philosophy," blackening and discrediting everyone who got in their way. In this manner, they established a "literary monopoly" and censorious control over the life of the mind. In a truly inimitable phrase, Burke observed with striking accuracy that these "atheistical fathers have a bigotry of their own; and they have learnt to talk against monks with the spirit of the monk." As the political philosopher Leo Strauss once put it, they partook in and radicalized "the anti-theological ire" typical of theoretical modernity as a whole. Burke accurately predicted that their "intolerance of the tongue and the pen" would readily give rise to an active "persecution which would strike at property, liberty, and life." No one saw more acutely the totalitarian logic inherent in politicized atheism and a secular religion dedicated to "remaking men and societies at a stroke," in the words of a great twentieth-century critic of secular religion Raymond Aron. Burke was the first to see that politicized atheism and murderous ideological despotism went hand in hand.

In contrast to the new revolutionary fanaticism, Burke appealed to the decency and sobriety of the English people, a decency rooted in the conviction that "religion is the basis of civil society" (all quotations in this paragraph are drawn from *RRF*, 77). If there are defects or corruptions in the established religion, the English "shall not call on atheism to explain them." They prefer even superstition to atheism. Burke's Christianity, his religious affirmation, is rooted in deference to the Most High, a deep and abiding respect for the moral law, and a tolerance of all the great expressions of Christianity, the Greek, the Armenian, and even the Roman (Burke revealingly adds "since heats are subsided"). Perhaps more than the English as a whole, Burke combines tolerance to all the great families within the Christian religion (and other religions such as the Hindu) with "zeal," not "indifference" toward truth and the moral law. There is no evidence that Burke ever saw the Christian religion merely as a crucial edifice at the heart of a free and decent political order even if it was assuredly that too. He was a theist and Christian by conviction but one shorn of all fanaticism, religious or secular.

The Essence of Jacobinism

Even after the juridical execution of Robespierre in the summer of 1794 (on the ninth of Thermidor in the revolutionary year 2), Burke continued to see the French revolution, in its various permutations, as essentially "Jacobin" in character. Its foundations were built on regicide, the execution of the king and queen; on atheism and fanatical opposition to the Christian religion in any recognizable or orthodox form; and on a new system of manners rooted in cruelty and desecration of everything sacred and holy. In a beautiful passage in the *First Letter on a Regicide Peace* (1796), Burke calls the revolutionaries (of all stripes) "regicide(s) by establishment" since they see monarchy, anywhere and everywhere, as nothing but a usurpation. Burke was appalled that the revolutionaries, even as they abolished "every festival of [true] religion," chose "the most flagrant act of a murderous regicide treason for a feast of eternal commemoration." These men respected no limits, no traditions, and they acknowledged no enduring and immutable sacred restraints. They were thus indeed "regicides by establishment" who made murder one of their founding principles.

Equally, revolutionaries of all stripes declared war on the traditional property of France and added to their legacy endless crimes and confiscations. But as Conor Cruise O'Brien has noted, unlike the Marxist-Leninists, they did not aim to abolish property as such. In that sense, their totalitarianism turned out to be less thoroughgoing, and in the end, less murderous than that carried out by the Bolsheviks in the Soviet Union or the Maoists in Communist China. Lastly, Burke saw even in the France of the allegedly more moderate Directory that succeeded Robespierre the same "atheism by establishment" that refused to truly recognize "God as a moral regulator of the world." The revolutionaries still aimed, if more prudently, "to abolish the Christian religion by a regular decree." In place of the social benevolence of the Christian religion and its salutary calls for self-denial, Burke saw "indecent theatric rites" at the service of "their vitiated, perverted reason" and sacrilegious altars to their "own corrupted and bloody republic." Accompanying all this was a terrible degeneration of manners and morals with more than isolated examples of *cannibalism*, where revolutionaries drank the blood of their victims, so-called "enemies of the people." In these displays, Burke saw sacrilege, impiety, and a demonic assault on sacred limits and restraints. Such deeds were "unmanly" and "abominable" in Burke's estimation, incompatible with both true liberty and civilization.[3]

All this led Burke to conclude that Robespierre's allegedly more moderate successors were regicides, fanatics, and atheists in their own right. As Burke wrote in the *Fourth Letter on a Regicide Peace* from 1795, the "present rulers" of France had done everything to enable Robespierre's cruel despotism: "He was a Tyrant, they were his satellites and his hangmen." In a grand and devastating rhetorical flourish, Burke adds, "They have expiated their other murders by a new murder. It has always been the case among the banditti." Perhaps Burke in the end underestimated the prospects for the return to something like a normal society in France. The Jacobins, strictly speaking, ruled France for less than two years, and the French revolution was less totalitarian than the Bolshevik regime would turn out to be since the Soviet assault on religion, traditional morality, and property was significantly more thoroughgoing than that of the French Revolutionaries. But it was the most "revolutionary" experience that the world had seen to date.

But one can hardly quarrel with Burke's claim that the enemy of Britain and the civilized world was not historic France but an "armed doctrine" that had conquered and warred on the France that was an integral part of European and Christian civilization. For that reason, Burke concluded in his 1794 "Preface to Bris-

---

3 Views shared by Alexander Hamilton, if not by Thomas Paine (who traveled to revolutionary France out of deep ideological sympathy and ended up in a Jacobin jail for advocating clemency for the king and the royal family) or Thomas Jefferson (who never truly saw the French Revolution for the evil it was and became). Hamilton, in contrast, loathed any moral identification of the American cause with that of revolutionary France. In a private text from 1794, Hamilton called the French revolutionaries "fanatics in politics science" who propagated "theories of government unsuited to the nature of man." He saw at the heart of the new system a murderous "impiety and infidelity" unworthy of a free and Christian people. See Hamilton, "Views of the French Revolution, 1794" in *The Political Writings of Alexander Hamilton*, Volume 2: 1789–1804, edited by Carson Holloway and Bradford P. Wilson (Cambridge University Press, 2017), pp. 233–34.

sot's Address to his Constituents" (Brissot was a regicide and a supporter of the Directory) that "neutrality" was not an option in dealing with revolutionary France. Jacobinism in the largest sense of the term "cannot be viewed with indifference." In a peak of rhetorical exuberance, Burke writes that this demonic system "must be regarded either with enthusiastic admiration, or with the highest degree of detestation, resentment, and horror." This is precisely the judgment that Solzhenitsyn would hold in regard to Soviet totalitarianism, an "armed doctrine" at war with humanity, religion, and decency and thoroughly destructive of liberty and human dignity. Burke was the first thinker and statesman to discern the true nature of ideological despotism. This is among his greatest insights and contributions to Western political thought.

Comparing Two Revolutions

The conservative sociologist Robert Nisbet has observed that Burke saw that "France under the Jacobins was 'exactly like a country of conquest.'" Nisbet adds that the American revolutionaries, in contrast, self-consciously limited "arbitrary power." Nisbet adds: "The American Revolution had sought freedom for actual, living human beings and their customs and habits." The French Revolutionaries, in marked contrast, promoted "leveling in the name of equality, nihilism in the name of liberty, and power, absolute power and total, in the name of the people" while having contempt for real human beings and inherited traditions and rights. Nisbet points out that one of Burke's most discerning insights was to see that the Jacobins, again capaciously understood, "were willing to destroy all institutions that interfered with the making of Revolutionary Man." And "their manifest wish" was "to extend the work of the Revolution to all of Europe, eventually to the world." Burke was thus right to discern totalitarianism in the French Revolution, but he perhaps overestimated how complete this totalitarianism would or could be in practice. That completion would wait until the twentieth century. But as Russell Kirk, another great twentieth-century Burkean has argued, the "crying need" of the twentieth century became the need "to avert revolutions, not to multiply them." As Kirk adds, "revolution," so understood, "is no highroad to life, liberty, and the pursuit of happiness." Only after the inhuman chimera of total revolution is rejected can conservative reform do its humanizing work. Political reason, prudence, the "god of this lower world," can then take its rightful place in the affairs of men.

Taking Aim at Applied "Theory"

Edmund Burke is the statesman and political philosopher par excellence who took aim at the effort "to reconstruct whole societies 'upon a theory.'" As Conor Cruise O'Brien (whom I have just quoted) rightly adds, the "three great revolutions of the twentieth century"—Soviet, Nazi, and Maoist—have confirmed Burke's warnings "on an awesome scale" (O'Brien in *RRF*, 231). In warning against the ideological temptation, Burke was "at the same time liberal and counter-revolutionary," as the French political theorist Philippe Raynaud has succinctly put it (O'Brien in *RRF*, 226–27). The great and perspicacious Anglo-Irish statesman saw himself as a friend of liberty, a caretaker of a tradition of liberty that required prudent statesmanship and, at times, toughminded conservative reform. Limitless revolutions, in contrast, aiming at total innovation and the destruction of the civic and moral inheritance passed on by our forebears, could only result in what O'Brien has called "successive mutations of despotism" (O'Brien in *RRF*, 230–31).

Prudence, Not Cultural or Moral Relativism

The abstract theorizing of the French revolutionaries (and its intellectual boosters) that Burke excoriated should not be confused with any contempt for truth or enduring moral principles on his part. Burke is the furthest thing from a relativist or a historicist who denies unchanging truths. In the impeachment trial of Warren Hastings, the governor general of the East India Company, for governing India in the spirit of a rapacious conquering army, Burke famously criticized "geographical morality." He insisted that "the laws of morality are the same everywhere; and actions that are stamped with the character of peculation, extortion, oppression, and barbarity in England, are so in Asia, and the world over." The Burke scholar Peter Stanlis has persuasively argued that Burke remained in some sense an adherent (although I would add a qualified one) of the natural law tradition. A moral and cultural relativist he was not.

"The science of constructing a commonwealth, or renovating it, or reforming it, is, like every other experimental science, not to be taught à priori" (*RRF*, 51). It nonetheless needs to be guided by wisdom rooted in historical experience, carefully crafted prudential judgment, and the moral precepts shared by all decent and civilized peoples. Political reason, Burke tells us, "is a computing principle; adding, subtracting, multiplying, and dividing, morally and not metaphysically, or mathematically, true moral denominations" (*RRF*, 52). If political reason so understood eschews the spirit of abstraction, of reckless theorizing, if it does not confuse metaphysical certitude with the necessarily "circumstantial" character of

political judgment, it nonetheless deals with "true moral denominations." Unless directed by sound principles or even by "prejudice,"
understood by Burke as deference to the practical *wisdom* inherent
in long-established traditions, circumstances in and of themselves
cannot determine the decisions of a statesman. Prudence needs
principle as much as principle needs prudence. Guided by the classics such as Aristotle and Cicero, Burke never confuses prudence
with mere calculation or pragmatism or with a rejection of moral
limits and constraints. In this regard, he is with the ancients and the
Christians and not the modern Machiavellian tradition.

Political reason is thus a practical or non-metaphysical manifestation of the human capacity for reason and has nothing to do with
a rejection of reason per se. Tradition is indispensable to political
reason precisely because it is a powerful vehicle for passing on the
inherited or tried-and-true wisdom of the human race. It is in no
way a "mystical" or irrational substitute for theoretical or practical
reason. Rather, it is the form reason takes in the judgments and
decisions appropriate to the changing circumstances that consti-
tute public life and the great tasks of public-spirited statesmanship. Burke is a critic of an all-encompassing political rationalism
but never of political reason within its legitimate sphere.

Prudence as Tough-Minded Moderation

As Greg Weiner puts it in his fine, recent book *Old Whigs: Burke,
Lincoln, and the Politics of Prudence,* the prudent statesman must
learn to combine "principle and circumstance" and, I would add,
moderation and courage in a judicious and prudent way. Those
noble virtues have an essential place in the exercise of judgment
and action informed by prudence and are virtues in and of themselves. Weiner expertly shows that, for Burke, prudence is insep-

arably connected to "politic caution, a guarded circumspection" and a "moral rather than complexional timidity." Those qualities, Burke wrote, were always "among the ruling principles of our forefathers in their most decided conduct." Weiner quite rightly remarks that Burke "was perhaps the first commentator fully to theorize the case for caution as a sort of default position rooted in the moral virtue of humility." The statesman is first and foremost the caretaker of a noble (if imperfect) inheritance that must be safeguarded and even cherished. Precipitous and presumptuous efforts to depart from the tried and true woefully exaggerate the human capacity to begin things de novo, from scratch, without the guidance of the wisdom of the past or the experience of our forebears. Burke's endorsement of "politic caution" is thus both practical and epistemological in character since the revolutionary "innovator" has little or no appreciation of what he does not know. From this fatal mixture of ignorance and hubris only reckless destruction can follow.

But once the ideological temptation is afoot in the human world, moderation must be accompanied by courage and no inconsiderable amount of spiritedness if civilization is to survive. When many in the English political class mistook post-Robespierre France with an ordinary European power, pursuing its national interest like any other great people or nation, Burke took aim at a "misguided prudence" that confused cowardice (or confusion) with humility. Burke saw "imprudent timidity" all around him rather than the true "wisdom of a nation." Confronted by an aggressive ideological despotism that aimed to upend all governments not based on its revolutionary principles, Burke attacked the "unworthy hesitation" that flowed from the lack of "the courage to see" (to use a phrase of Solzhenitsyn's addressing a similar tendency among twentieth-century politicians and intellectuals who refused to acknowledge expansionist Communism for what it really was). Weiner draws our attention to a distinction Burke introduces in the *Letters on a Regicide Peace* between "courageous wisdom" and a "false, reptile prudence" that arises not out of salutary "caution" but out of "fear" and misjudgment perhaps rooted in the failure to cultivate "the courage to see." Yet whether as an advocate of "politic caution" or as a critic of "hesitating prudence" and "weakness of will," Burke continues to exercise all the humanizing arts of prudence. In addition, his appeal to courage is never severed from an underlying moderation committed to the preservation of a civilization that bows in gratitude before the inherited wisdom of the past and that upholds the permanent necessity of "sacred limits and restraints." Of all the thinking statesmen who are highlighted in this book, few match the capaciousness of Burke's soul, one that ties together courage and moderation and nobility of spirit with a humble deference before both God and the great inheritance that is civilization itself. Burke exudes nobility in his every thought and deed.

Reason and Justice Versus the Emancipated Will

Burke made one other vital contribution, both theoretical and practical, that is generally little noted or appreciated. He was the first and greatest critic of the "emancipation of the will" from natural and divine superintendence. That emancipation, with its accompanying tendency to conflate legitimate authority with authoritarianism and to reduce all obligations to freely chosen ones (hence the omnipresence of "consent" in modern moral and political discourse) is paradoxically coextensive with moral anarchy and the worst forms of political despotism. Like Tocqueville, Guizot, and Bertrand de Jouvenel after him, Burke understood that the "regulated will" tied to a "manly, moral, regulated liberty," as he called it at the beginning of *Reflections*, is the only liberty that is truly in accord with the moral nature of human beings and the sempiternal requirements of the public good. The unregulated will is the principle, if one deigns to call it that, of anarchy and despotism and never of civilized or ordered liberty. This insight is at the core of all subsequent anti-totalitarian wisdom.

As early as his "Letter to Charles-Jean-François Depont" from November 1789, Burke expressed some inchoate reservations about the course of the then relatively new French Revolution. He already saw a dangerous elevation of an unhindered and inebriated "will" as the animating force behind the revolutionaries. The people were sovereign, the nation was sovereign, and increasingly the Revolution itself was sovereign. These new entities or powers bowed before nothing or anything. No limits—political, historical, customary, spiritual—were to get in the way of the Great Emancipation and Transformation that they imagined. The revolutionaries had set will "above reason and justice" (and in a profound sense, Burke believed in the sovereignty of "right reason," as both Cicero and the Christian tradition called it). This emancipation of the will at the heart of ideological revolution—and the French Revolution was the world's first ideological revolution if one less complete than the ideological revolutions of the twentieth century—allowed the French to make "a revolution, but not a reformation." Writing to Depont, Burke said of the French: "You may have subverted monarchy, but not recovered freedom." Burke knew that lawlessness, terror, violence, and murderous impiety flowed inexorably from this blind rejection of the "regulated will." The French had crossed a moral and political Rubicon into a new territory where moral nihilism and brutal despotism reigned.

Burke had nothing but contempt for those who were shamelessly giddy before such a display.

Unsought Obligations and the Limits of Consent

A few years later, in *An Appeal from the New to the Old Whigs* (1791), his stirring defense of traditional Whig principles against their revolutionary subversion by Charles Fox and other Whig sympathizers with the French Revolution, Burke deepened his argument. Consent plays some role in the defining of political obligations, but duty, the opposite of will, in truth owes little to consent. Obligations arise out of the very nature of human association itself and are rarely the product of "any special voluntary pact." Even when obligations begin in free choice, as with marriage in the Christian West, the resulting duties to spouse and children "are all compulsive." A decent and lawful human being cannot and should not opt out of them. Likewise, multiple obligations arise out of "the relation of man to man, and the relation of man to God." Men of true liberty and true virtue must honor these obligations because without them our humanity (and our freedom) withers. Burke's conservative-minded liberalism has no place for our regnant illusions about individual or collective autonomy, a conceit that enslaves human beings under the pretext of making them gods. Liberty is always "liberty under God and the laws," to quote a piquant formulation from Alexis de Tocqueville from the third part of *The Old Regime and the Revolution*. About this, Burke and Tocqueville are in complete agreement.

The French Revolution and radical modernity more broadly involved not only an assault on what Burke called "compulsive obligations," ones that are truly obligatory regardless of one's choice or consent, but an equally fundamental attack on the man-

ners and morals that constituted the European inheritance at its
very best. It was this assault, evident already in the summer and
fall of 1789, that alerted Burke to the essentially destructive, tyrannical, and even nihilistic character of the French Revolution. As
we shall see in the next chapter, later French liberals, even conservative-minded ones such as Alexis de Tocqueville and François
Guizot, defended the "principles of 1789" while emphatically criticizing the Revolution's later degeneration into terror and mob
rule. They excoriated "1793" while defending, if in a qualified and
not wholly convincing way, the original "noble" intentions of the
revolutionaries.

Burke, in contrast, condemned the revolution *tout court* as an
unqualified disaster from its inception. As many scholars have
observed, Burke at first adopted a wait-and-see attitude, skeptical but open to the possibility that the French Revolution would
culminate, in fits and starts, in ordered liberty and constitutional
monarchy. A few of the original revolutionaries after all, *Monar-
chiens* such as Jean Joseph Mounier, esteemed the English constitution and hoped for moderate and stable political arrangements
in France that did not break definitively or absolutely with the
old French monarchy. But these admirers of Montesquieu and
English liberty (the two admirations went hand in hand) were
already outmaneuvered in the National Assembly by the beginning of August 1789. They would have no influence to speak of
on the subsequent evolution of an ever more self-radicalizing revolutionary movement and process. But it was the events of October 6, 1789, the brutal and hitherto unimaginable assault on the
king and queen at Versailles and their involuntary return to Paris
as prisoners of a Parisian mob that confirmed Burke's worst sus-
picions about the French Revolution. Henceforth, he would be
its most astute, eloquent, fierce, and determined opponent. And

in rallying all his analytic and rhetorical powers to oppose (and expose) the proto-totalitarianism of the French Revolution, Burke would outline a modern conservative political philosophy at once liberal, anti-totalitarian, and counterrevolutionary.

The Eruption of Revolutionary Nihilism: The Events of October 6, 1789

Burke's eloquent and forceful critique of the events of October 6, 1789, goes to the heart of his critique of revolutionary fanaticism and of the liberal conservatism he would limn in response to it. On the morning of the sixth, "a band of cruel ruffians and assassins," as Burke called them, murdered the sentinel guarding Queen Marie Antoinette's bedroom door at Versailles, waving their bayonets and going in search of more blood to spill. The "splendid" royal palace at Versailles was, in Burke's dramatic words, "left swimming in blood, polluted by massacre, and strewed with scattered limbs and mutilated carcases" (all quotations in this paragraph are drawn from *RRF*, 60–61). Burke found this spectacle appalling in every respect. King Louis XVI, Marie Antoinette, and their infant children were effectively made captives who were forcibly "conducted into the capital of their kingdom." Two of the king's bodyguards "were cruelly and publicly dragged to the block," and their heads were then placed on bobbing spears to head the forced procession to Paris and to intimidate the royal family. Burke describes with genuine disgust "the horrid yells, and shrilling screams, and frantic dances" that accompanied this slow, torturous "journey of twelve miles" back to Paris.

A civilized and mannered people were now at the mercy of an inhuman, bloodthirsty mob. New rituals of desecration were now the order of the day. The twentieth-century French political philosopher Bertrand de Jouvenel has persuasively argued that Burke's violent and vehement opposition to the French Revolution owes everything to his genuine shock at "the new expressions on faces, the new tone of voices" that emanated from the violent nihilistic French revolutionary mob. They were inebriated by blood and a new revolutionary ideology that put audacity and shameless-ness before all. As Jouvenel wrote in a marvelous passage from the chapter on "The Manner of Politics" in his 1963 book, *The Pure Theory of Politics*, "When the mob marched to Versailles and carried the Royal family with it by mere pressure of force, when the heads of guards, carried on spears, were kept bobbing up and down at the windows of the Queen's carriage, this outrage, both to formality and sensitivity, was one which the deputies dare not condemn, and it is apparent in Burke's writing that such a scene and its condoning by the assembly swayed him altogether."[4] One could not say it better. The events of October 6, 1789, displayed a new barbarism at war with both decency and civilized manners. The barbarians were literally at the gates, and the common Euro-pean home was under threat.

Burke's fierce reaction to these angry faces and loud voices and to the violence and mayhem that accompanied them, as well his great paean that follows to the memory of the then dauphiness of France at Versailles sixteen or seventeen years before in all her resplendent glory, has nothing to do with foolish romanticism, as some have claimed. Burke recalls the dignified "elevation" of the future queen of France and the "gallant men" who surrounded her to remind his readers how far the French had fallen in just a few months since their revolution had begun. It is this memory and reflection that gives rise to Burke's famous lament that "the age of chivalry is gone.

4 Bertrand de Jouvenel, *The Pure Theory of Politics*, Foreword by Daniel J. Ma-honey (Indianapolis, IN: Liberty Fund, 2000), 252.

That of sophisters, economists, and calculators, has succeeded; and the glory of Europe is extinguished forever" (*RRF*, 65).

The Spirit of Chivalry and the "Unbought Grace of Life"

Burke was no enemy of modern commerce or of the economic arts that gave rise to the prosperity of European peoples. He was a friend and admirer of Adam Smith, the author of *The Wealth of Nations* (1776), the most significant modern philosophical defense of the market and the "system of natural liberty." But Burke was above all a partisan of the "unbought grace of life." He did not see how even modern liberty could survive (and flourish) without some degree of "manly sentiment and heroic enterprise."[5] If the spirit of chivalry and personal honor—informed by valor, gentlemanliness, and self-restraint—were ever "totally extinguished, the loss [I] fear," Burke writes in this famous passage, "will be great." Burke so eloquently defended "all the pleasing illusions, which made power gentle and obedience liberal" precisely because the "decent drapery of life" (which the revolutionaries were prepared to so brutally tear off) raised human beings (and societies) above "the defects of our naked, shivering nature." "The new conquering empire of light and reason" propagated by the *philosophes* and brutally realized by the revolutionary mob, was not so reasonable after all. True human reason "ratifies" what Burke calls the "moral imagination" (for these quotations see *RRF*, 65–66) since the manners and morals that inform it are inseparable from the

---

5 Burke's genuine sympathy with the emerging market order combined with an equally adamant refusal to reduce civilization to commercial prosperity and "transnational exchanges" is brilliantly and comprehensively explored in Gregory M. Collins, *Commerce and Manners in Edmund Burke's Political Economy* (Cambridge, UK, and New York: Cambridge University Press, 2020). This learned, balanced, and well-written book fills a pressing need in Burke scholarship. See the fuller discussion of it in the second part of this chapter.

only liberty, civilized or ordered liberty, worthy of human beings. Manners and morals, so understood, are a precious acquisition of Western and European civilization. It was Burke, long before the "gentlemen" that he defended, who saw exactly what was at stake when these great goods came under determined nihilistic assault. Burke was truly *defensor civitatis* in the manner of Cicero or Churchill. In him, all the cardinal virtues—courage, temperance, prudence, and justice—are richly on display.

The Grandeur—and Limits—of Gentlemanly Prudence

The political philosopher Harvey C. Mansfield, a prominent Burke scholar among the other impressive intellectual hats he wears, has reminded us that Burke, the great "champion of gentlemanly prudence," saw through the considerable limits of the gentlemen class he so nobly defended. Too many of these soi-disant gentlemen and nobles, like his allies in the Whig Party he had so well served, "could not see the difference between the American Revolution and the French," something Burke could so readily do, and with all the appropriate distinctions. Burke saw what they could not see: that the French revolution was "the most complete revolution ever known." Burke chose to defend an "actual constitution," a tolerably and even admirably free one, against the impatience and incipient fanaticism of an emerging intellectual class. As Mansfield notes, his gentlemen are no more. But they, and we, have found no adequate substitute for them. In a striking formulation, Mansfield notes that the gentleman is defined by everything that is lacking in all our substitutes for them—among them bureaucrats, technocrats, and democrats. One might add that Burke, in his Sisyphean efforts to defend the gentleman from his occasional shortsightedness and imprudence, fulfilled one of the essential practical tasks of the public-spirited political philosopher as defined by Leo Strauss: to defend sound practice against bad or pernicious theory. In a world overrun by the ideological thinking Burke so despised, that task remains a preeminent one for political philosophy, rightly understood.

The Burke Who Can Still Speak to Us

In that regard, Burke very much remains our contemporary. But excessively traditionalist or romantic readings and appropriations of Burke are bound to fail because they tie his genuinely enduring insights to *a society in transition* from the old regime to the world of modern liberty (and despotism) that is no longer ours. But as the great French conservative liberal Raymond Aron wrote in a sparkling essay from 1957 about "Conservatism in Industrial Societies," Burke's work serves as a permanent and salutary reminder that the true liberal seeks to conserve a civilization that is broader and deeper than the "abstract moralism" proffered by the adherents of the contemporary ideology of the rights of man. Prudence, and not ideology or a unilateral emphasis on rights claims unaccompanied by duties and public spiritedness, remains the principal virtue of free political life, of the arts of noble citizenship and statesmanship. Burke is best understood today, Aron adds, as the most illuminating critic of ideological fanaticism and not of reason or rationalism per se. Rather than reading the great Anglo-Irish statesman as a defender of the now antiquated hierarchies of the French and European old regimes, we should continue to draw on his insight "that all society implies a hierarchy and only prospers in the reciprocal respect of rights and duties." Burke is best approached not as an enemy of democracy, especially of a sober or restrained sort, but as the great statesman-theorist of "wisdom" (*sagesse* in French) that is of high moral and political prudence in the tradition of Aristotle and Cicero. So understood, he remains an indispensable thinker and statesman. Burke's delicate mixture of statesmanship and political philosophy, of classical liberalism and classical conservatism, will continue to "be cherished as long as any one survives in the world who has a perception of true liberty," as Irving Babbitt put it so well in his classic work *Democracy and Leadership* in 1924.

Rousseau versus Burke, and "Benevolence" versus True Virtue

Burke has one more vital thing to teach us. He is the first and still unparalleled critic of "the philosophy of vanity," as he called it in the *Letter to a Member of the National Assembly* (1791), a philosophy and personal bearing emblematically represented, he famously tells us, by that "insane Socrates," Jean-Jacques Rousseau. Unlike many later soi-disant Burkeans, Burke himself appreciated the genius and some of the insights of Rousseau the philosopher and writer. But he faulted him for his endless self-obsession, his preoccupation with his "mad faults," and the way he made "openness and candour" and a rather histrionic "benevolence" the whole of virtue. In this new account of the model man, sentimentality substituted for order in the soul and love of humanity for respect for the rights, dignity, and obligations of real human beings. Daniel Ritchie has pointed out a striking passage in Burke's June 1, 1791, letter to Chevalier Claude François de Rivarol where the English statesman links this pseudo-benevolence to a "polluted atheism" that "flatter(s)" the passions of the young, "natural and unnatural." Facile humanitarianism or "benevolence," divorced from every effort to "restrain the appetite," leads to a frightful state of soul beyond "good or evil." As Ritchie provocatively puts it, Burke took aim at an alleged "inalienable right to expand the empire of unnatural vices." His appeal to the "moral imagination" in *Reflections* and elsewhere is also an attack on a "diabolical imagination" where wisdom, self-restraint, salutary tradition and sound prejudice, and even the elementary and primordial distinction between good and evil ultimately have no place. As the prophet and theorist of a humane "moral imagination," Burke provides us with the wherewithal and the inspiration to free ourselves from the regnant nihilism that wars with the nature and needs of the human soul, especially the precious *imago dei* that marks man as man and is the ultimate source of human dignity. Burke, the statesman and thinker, appeals to and draws upon the best classical and Christian wisdom in his noble effort to defend true liberty against ideological assaults.

―――――

Giving Virtue and Commercial Liberty Their Due: Burke on the Place and Limits of Political Economy

Is there a "Das Edmund Burke Problem" to match or accompany the "Das Adam Smith Problem" discovered, or invented, by German scholars from the mid-nineteenth century onward? The latter problem, as defined by these German savants, centered on the alleged contradiction between *The Wealth of Nations*'s marked emphasis on economic self-interest as a crucial vehicle in expanding the prosperity of modern peoples and the vital place of sympathy (and the moral sense and moral virtues more broadly) in Smith's equally fundamental work *The Theory of Moral Sentiments*. The transformation of a tension and a due regard for the complexity inherent in reality into an intractable "problem" has dogged scholarship on Adam Smith ever since, although the best scholars now see tension-ridden complementarity rather than any real opposition between Smith's economic theory and his moral philosophy. In his groundbreaking recent work *Commerce and Manners in Edmund Burke's Political Economy*[6], Gregory M. Collins deflates a pseudo–Edmund Burke problem in a way that richly illuminates and clarifies Burke's unique mixture of classical liberalism, moral traditionalism, and a conservative-minded politics of prudence. One cannot do justice to Burke's political reflection and his unique approach to political economy without giving due place to both a modernist appreciation of the laws of commerce and a half-traditionalist emphasis on virtue, manners, and the robustly social nature of human beings. In this task of clarification, Collins succeeds brilliantly.

So much of the supposed "Edmund Burke Problem" stems from a singular preoccupation with *Thoughts and Details on Scarcity* (1796), his major economic tract published five years after *Reflections on the Revolution in France*. As Collins ably demonstrates, it is in no way surprising that, in the latter work, Burke continues to defend "the inviolability of property" and "the belief that the natural order sanctioned the free diffusion of commerce" (*CM*, 2). These were long established convictions of Burke the statesman, political philosopher, and political economist. What is striking, even perplexing, for some is that Burke, the grandiloquent critic of the spirit of abstraction in politics and political thought, resists government intervention in the domestic grain trade (in

6 Gregory M. Collins, *Commerce and Manners in Edmund Burke's Political Economy* (Cambridge, UK, and New York, New York: Cambridge University Press, 2020). The "Das Problem Adam Smith" is discussed particularly well on p. 5. All subsequent references to the Collins book will be cited parenthetically in the body of the text as *CM* followed by the appropriate page number or numbers.

a time of acute shortages) on the grounds of abstract and rationalist principles rather than in the prudential or circumstantial mode familiar to the readers of *Reflections*. Burke famously goes further in *Thoughts and Details on Scarcity* by identifying the "laws of commerce" with "the laws of nature, and consequently the laws of God." This "invocation of general principles," as Collins calls it, seems to exude the spirit of abstraction (*CM*, 2).

But this single work and single quotation does not exhaust Burke's infinitely more capacious approach to political economy. As Collins demonstrates, Burke, like Friedrich A. Hayek well after him, had ample reasons—theoretical and practical, civic and moral—to oppose efforts by governing authorities to set prices in the grain or any other market in a way that distorted the information about goods and services, and market preferences, that only a competitive market order adequately makes available to producers and consumers alike.[7] Neither Burke nor Hayek were wrong in insisting that in Collins's deft formulation "the locus of epistemological authority in exchange economies should reside in those immediately involved in producing, consuming, and trading, since the mysterious motions of commerce were too elusive to be fully understood by fallible men in power" (*CM*, 137). When such interventions in the market and pricing system begin, it is very difficult, if not impossible, to extricate oneself from them. Still, on classically Burkean grounds, such theoretical judgments must be subject to the high tribunal of prudential judgment and circumstantial wisdom. The famous formulation that the "laws of commerce" were coextensive with the "laws of nature" and the "laws of God" goes too far. It is inflexible in a most un-Burkean way. But as Collins shows, Burke was no heartless Social Darwinian avant la lettre. He

---

7 Roger Scruton has made this comparison between Burke and Hayek in many of his writings.

was generous to the poor around him, and at the end of his life he founded and helped fund a school for the children of dispossessed French émigrés. He even housed a French émigré family in a cottage on his property free of charge (*CM*, 536). This sometime political economist was a Christian of conviction and a man of goodwill. By all accounts, he was moved by generosity and by what Smith and the Scots would call sympathy towards those in need and by what Burke would more likely call *caritas*.

One of the great merits of Collins's book is that he never succumbs to the temptation to reduce Burke's great mind and soul to convenient but misleading abstractions and simplifications. Burke eloquently defended the place of landed property in a balanced political and social order, but at the same time he saw merit in mobile property and in the crucial role of middlemen in promoting commerce and trade. His "Speech on St. Eustatius" (1782) notably "defended the Jewish people" who lived on the island conquered from the Dutch by Britain "for their vital role in establishing an international network of communication channels and credit markets." These Jewish middlemen were, in Burke's memorable phrase, "the conductors by which credit was transmitted through the world" (*CM*, 62). But if Burke defended "elements of classical liberalism," in Collins's words, he was not a classical liberal per se (*CM*, 16). And while Burke defended virtue (and prudence) in a manner reminiscent of the classics and medievals, he did not share the premodern antipathy toward commerce and commercial acquisition. He was a partisan of the market economy but a critic of the effort to reduce the whole of human life to economic criteria. Like the best (liberal) conservatives in the modern age, he wished to integrate "the pursuit of profit with the ethical preconditions of freedom" (*CM*, 16). Burke was committed to harmonizing as much as possible liberty (including commercial liberty) and virtue without succumbing to utopianism or nostalgia for romanticized conceptions of ancient liberty (Sparta or early republican Rome) à la Rousseau.

As a Christian and an eminently civilized human being, Burke rejected the notion that everything could or should be brought to the market. He loathed slavery and the slave trade, and he drafted a "Sketch of a Negro Code" in 1780 to put the slave trade on the road to "incremental abolition." He made the "Code" public in 1792, and it "made a favorable impression upon William Wilberforce, the great anti-slavery campaigner" (*CM*,56–57). Burke believed, in his own words, that the abolition of the slave trade would be in accord with "the principles of true religion and morality" (*CM*, 57). He wanted to regulate the slave trade out of existence, making it so costly that, in Collin's formulation, "it would smother the incentive to deal Africans." His "Sketch of a Negro Code" would also give slaves "the liberties to acquire and inherit property, pursue educational and employment opportunities, and take time off from labor for religious worship" (*CM*, 57). A gradualist and not a strict abolitionist, Burke nonetheless hated slavery as much as Tocqueville and Lincoln after him. His "Code," in effect, would go a long way to blurring any meaningful distinction between slave and non-slave. It is an admirable illustration of Burkean prudence and gradualism at work. Collins quotes a revealing speech of Burke's from May 1778 where the great statesman confessed that he was "no advocate for a trade which consisted, in the greatest measure, of men's bodies, and not of manufactures" (*CM*, 57). Collins's eloquent comment on this passage goes to the heart of the matter:

The natural laws of commerce should govern the circulation of material goods, but not the trafficking of human beings,

for slavery shocked the principles of humanity. Supply and demand stopped at the soul (*CM*, 57).

Burke was first and foremost an advocate for and practitioner of
"the humane economy," as Wilhelm Röpke famously called it in
1959 in a seminal book by that name.

There are many other riches in Collins's book. He demonstrates Burke's ferocious opposition to economic monopoly in
India where the East India Company, under Governor General
of Bengal Warren Hastings, put the traditional "landed interest"
up "to public auction!" (in Burke's words) in order to satisfy the
greed and lust for power of British officials (*CM*, 401). Burke did
not oppose empire per se, but he was appalled when it became,
as it had in late eighteenth-century India, coextensive with sheer
rapaciousness. The Indians of India had a right to see their best
traditions respected (Burke was moderately "multicultural" in that
regard). Commerce became mere lawlessness when it "threatened
to undermine the moral and cultural foundations" (*CM*, 401) of
a long-established political community. And unmitigated monopoly, too, violated "the laws of commerce."

Collins's chapter on Burke, the French Revolution, and political
economy is particularly engaging (*CM*, 405–59). In Britain, Burke
saw a judicious balancing of landed and mobile property that reinforced Britain's admirable constitution of liberty (*CM*, 417). In
revolutionary France, in contrast, Burke saw men of "enterprising
talents" (as he put it in the *First Letter on a Regicide Peace*) warring
cruelly on hereditary and ecclesiastical property (*CM*, 420). Much
of what Burke has to say about this unrelenting war on traditional
forms of property (and the violence and cruelty that accompanied
it) was perfectly on mark. But Burke perhaps did not reflect sufficiently on how central the "right of property" was to French revo-

lutionary theory and practice. We are a long way from Karl Marx, who in the second section of *The Communist Manifesto* wrote that Communism could be summed up in a single sentence: the abolition of private property. It is indeed the case that much of the traditional property of France was "divid[ed] amongst the people of no property," as Burke put it in the *First Letter on a Regicide Peace* (quoted in *CM*, 420). But as Tocqueville observed in his *Recollections* of the Revolution of 1848, those peasant proprietors were to become fierce enemies of socialism (and Communism) during the revolution of 1848 and, I would add, during the Paris Commune a generation later.[8] In different ways, Burke and the French revolutionaries (except for its most extremist factions) were paradoxically both defenders of private property and the inviolable "laws of commerce." Only later, with Babeuf and his "Conspiracy of the Equals" and then Marx and the Marxists, would European revolutionaries turn decisively against property in principle and practice.

Collins ends his thoughtful and comprehensive book by pointing out that Burke, the defender of commercial liberty as well as salutary tradition, did not belong to the school of *doux commerce*. For Burke, manners civilize human beings, but they are not primarily a product of commercial exchange or market activity. "Flourishing enterprise was an adornment of prosperous communities," but it was no substitute, in Collins's apt formulation, for "the traditions of the past, social bonds of affection, an ethical foundation, cultural renewal, religious piety, and a sense of honor." Burke moves beyond the classics by endorsing a legitimate place in a free and decent political order for "the principles of market exchange." But he is classical and Christian through and through in believing, as Collins puts it

---

8 See the discussion of the "June Days" in Alexis de Tocqueville, *Recollections: The French Revolution of 1848 and Its Aftermath*, translated by Arthur Goldhammer (Charlottesville, VA: University of Virginia Press, 2016).

so well, that if societies reduce all social relations to transactional exchanges based on consent, "the human essence will be crushed by the soft tyranny of temporary and convenient social partnerships." Moral and political obligations transcend voluntary contracts and "remain even after such contracts dissolve" (*CM, 509*). In highlighting these old but largely forgotten truths, Gregory Collins has allowed Edmund Burke, partisan of virtue and liberty, to speak with eloquence and insight to a new generation.

Sources and Suggested Readings

For Mary Ann Glendon's excellent discussion of Cicero and Burke as the two greatest figures in the Western tradition who excelled in both politics and philosophy, see Glendon, *The Forum and the Tower: How Scholars and Politicians Have Imagined the World, from Plato to Eleanor Roosevelt* (New York: Oxford University Press, 2011), p. 131.

Churchill's beautiful encomium to Burke can be found in the essay "Consistency in Politics" in Churchill, *Thoughts and Adventures*, edited with a new introduction by James W. Muller (Wilmington, DE: ISI Books, 2009), pp. 35–37. See Glendon's helpful discussion of Churchill's account of Burke in *The Forum and the Tower*, p. 148 and my own discussion in Daniel J. Mahoney, *The Conservative Foundations of the Liberal Order* (Wilmington, DE: ISI Books, 2010), p. 7.

For the discussion of the ingratitude and insouciance of the pro-Jacobin aristocrats the Duke of Bedford and the Earl of Lauderdale, see *Letter to a Noble Lord* (1796) in Burke, *Reflections on the Revolution in France and Other Writings*, edited and introduced by Jesse Norman (New York, London, Toronto: Everyman's Library, 2015), pp. 878–916. Henceforth cited as Norman, *RRFAOW*.

For the discussion of the continuing relevance of Burke's critique of "leveling ideology and totalist politics," see Daniel E. Ritchie, "Foreword" to *Edmund Burke: Appraisals and Applications* (New Brunswick, NJ: Transaction Publishers, 1990), pp. ix–xi. This volume is hereafter referred to as *EBAA*.

George Watson's 1984 essay "Burke's Conservative Revolution" stands out for its lucid and elegant grasp of Burke's support for humane conservative reform as opposed to the nihilistic drive for "total change." See Ritchie, *EBBA*, pp. 78–79, 82, 85.

For Burke's discussion of ideology or "armed doctrine," see *First Letter on a Regicide Peace* in Norman, *RRFAOW*, p. 851.

For the reference to the French Revolution as a "Revolution of doctrine and theoretick dogma," see *Thoughts on French Affairs* (December 1791) in Daniel E. Ritchie, ed., *Further Reflections on the Revolution in France* (Indianapolis, IN: Liberty Find, 1992), p. 208. This volume will henceforth be referred to as Ritchie, *FRRF*. For the reference to the two-fold revolutionary "Colossus," see Norman, *RRFAOW*, p. 851.

For Burke's magisterial dissection of "the essence of Jacobinism," see *First Letter on a Regicide Peace* in Norman, *RFRAOW*, pp. 855–56.

On the "cannibalism" practiced by the Jacobins, see *First Letter on a Regicide Peace* in Norman, *RRFAOW*, 860.

On the leaders of the French Directorate as "expiating their other murders by a new murder" and all other quotes from the *Fourth Letter on a Regicide Peace*, see *The Writings and Speeches of Edmund Burke*, Volume IX, I: *The Revolutionary War*, II: *Ireland*, edited by R. B. McDowell (New York: Oxford University Press, 1991), p. 84. Hereafter referred to as McDowell, *TWSEB*.

For the quotations from Burke's "Preface to Brissot's address to his Constituents," see *The Writings and Speeches of Edmund*

Burke, Volume VIII: *The French Revolution*, 1790–1794, edited by L. G. Mitchell (New York: New York: Oxford University Press, 1998), pp. 519–20.

The quotations from Nisbet and Kirk can be found in Richie, *EBAA*, pp. 278–79, 283 for Nisbet and pp. 100–01 for Kirk.

Burke's famous and forceful critique of merely "geographical morality" is cited in Peter Stanlis's essay on "Burke and the Natural Law" in Ritchie, *EBAA*, pp. 223–24.

My discussion of Burke and prudence is indebted to Greg Weiner, Chapter One, "'The God of This Lower World': Burke on Prudence" in Weiner, *Old Whigs: Burke, Lincoln, and the Politics of Prudence* (New York: Encounter Books, 2019), especially pp. 13, 17, and 18.

For Burke's splendid critique of the revolutionary effort to put will "above reason and justice," see "Letter to Charles-Jean-François Depont" in Ritchie, *FRRF*, 8, 12, 16.

See Burke's illuminating and elevating discussion of "unsought obligations" and the limits of consent in *An Appeal from the New to the Old Whigs* in Norman, *RRFAOW*, 700–01.

For Harvey C. Mansfield's luminous account of the radically insufficient modern substitutes for Burke's beloved if imperfect gentlemen, see Mansfield, "Edmund Burke" in *History of Political Philosophy*: Third Edition, edited by Leo Strauss and Joseph Cropsey (Chicago, IL: University of Chicago Press, 1987), pp. 707–08.

Raymond Aron's account of the two ways of reading Burke today can be found in "De la droite" in his book *Espoir et peur du siècle: Essais non-partisans* (Paris: Calmann-Lévy, 1957), p. 120.

For the multiple reasons why Burke will continue to be cherished by all those who will still love "true liberty," see Irving Babbitt, "Burke and the Moral Imagination" in Ritchie, *EBAA*, p. 206.

On Rousseauan "vanity" and the French philosopher's role as "the mad Socrates" of the French National Assembly, see Burke, *Letter to a Member of the National Assembly* (1791) in Norman, *RRFAOW*, 663.

For an insightful discussion of Burke's critique of the new "empire of unnatural vices," see Daniel E. Ritchie's "Foreword" to *EBAA*, p. ix.

To conclude, I will point out myself what many readers are likely to regard as the major defect of my book. It is not precisely tailored to anyone's point of view. In writing it, I had no intention of serving or opposing any party. I did not try to look at things differently from the parties, but I did try to see further. They busy themselves with tomorrow only, while I aimed to think about the future.

— Concluding lines of Alexis de Tocqueville's
Introduction to *Democracy in America*

Only freedom can effectively combat the flaws natural to societies of this type and keep them from sliding down a slippery slope. Only freedom can rescue citizens from the isolation in which the very independence of their condition has mired them. Only freedom can compel them to come together and warm each other's spirits through mutual exchange and persuasion and joint action in practical affairs. Only freedom can save them from the worship of Mammon and the petty vexations of their private business, enabling them to sense the constant presence of the nation above and alongside them. Only freedom can substitute higher, more powerful passions for the love of material comforts and supply ambition with goals more worthy than the acquisition of wealth. Only freedom, finally, can create the light by which it is possible to see and judge the vices and virtues of humankind.

—Alexis de Tocqueville, Foreword to
The Old Regime and the Revolution

4

TOCQUEVILLE:
DEMOCRACY WITHOUT DEMAGOGY,
LIBERTY WITH A MODICUM
OF GREATNESS

Alexis de Tocqueville is another outstanding example of a great-souled man who lived his life at the intersection of thought and action, a statesman-theorist who combined magnanimity and moderation with due attentiveness to the requirements of modern liberty. Under the Orléanist monarchy in France, the governing political order in that country between the revolutions of 1830 and 1848, Tocqueville was for many years a parliamentarian representing a district in his native Normandy. In that role, he eloquently defended liberal principles, vigorously opposed new manifestations of the revolutionary spirit, and tirelessly advocated salutary social reforms, including the extension of the suffrage and the end of slavery and the slave trade. He repeatedly called for the enlargement of the political sphere to include more than the propertied classes and a rather narrow and entrenched, if relatively humane and liberal, oligarchy. He was also foreign minister of France for five months during the short-lived Second Republic (1848–1851). In that role, he served under President Louis Napoléon, the nephew of the great Bonaparte, an "adventurer" he hardly admired. A thinker and statesman who embodied honorable (or noble) ambition, he nonetheless will be remembered first and foremost for his three masterworks, *Democracy in America* (1835–1840), *The Old Regime and the Revolution* (1856), and the *Souvenirs* or *Recollections*, posthumously published in 1893 (Tocqueville died from tuberculosis at the age of 54 in 1859). In contradistinction to many other figures discussed in this book, we might more accurately call Tocqueville "the thinker as statesman" and not the other way around.

Between Thought and Action

In a revealing letter written to his cousin Louis de Kergorlay on December 15, 1850, a letter where Tocqueville outlined his thoughts and plans for the work that would become *The Old Regime and the Revolution*, Tocqueville freely acknowledged that his "true worth is above all in works of the mind; that [he is] worth more in thought than in action." He had a true gift for sketching ("painting" as he metaphorically called it) and comparing political "wholes" and, at the same time, for eschewing narrow partisanship and utopian political schemes. Above all, in his own self-understanding, he had but one great cause, "that of liberty and human dignity" against all the myriad parties, regimes, and ideologies that threatened them in the emerging democratic age.

His virtues and values were in many instances indistinguishable from those of Burke, but he was fully committed to ennobling democracy, not burying it. Burke, to be sure, was deeply dedicated to the cause of ordered liberty. But he could hardly imagine a truly free and decent political order that was in decisive respects "democratic." Pure democracy was for Burke indistinguishable from despotism. In contrast, Tocqueville saw a potential for "greatness" in democracy but only if it were informed by liberty and virtue. In addition, Tocqueville had a more complicated relationship to the legacy of the French Revolution than his Anglo-Irish predecessor. The revolution had become a crucial part of France's political heritage, and so Tocqueville felt obliged to distinguish its "opening act," where "love of equality" still "coexisted...with love of liberty" from both Jacobin and Napoleonic despotism. At the beginning of the revolution at least, Tocqueville discerned "generous and sincere passions" and not merely the seeds of unprecedented forms of despotism.[2]

Joseph Epstein, in his small but compelling biography of Tocqueville,[3] wryly asks what the great Frenchman himself would have made of "le phénomène de Tocqueville" (*E*,1). For as Epstein points out, it is impossible nowadays to think "about America, about democracy, about liberty, about bureaucracy, about equality, about almost any aspect of politics, or for that matter about large stretches of human nature" (*E*, 1) without reference to Tocqueville. Yet there is, in truth, no simple answer to Epstein's question because the philosopher, statesman, and political thinker Toc-

---

1 In a letter to Pierre Freslon dated September 11, 1857, Tocqueville wrote that what saddened him was not democracy per se but only a "democratic society without liberty." He could not imagine anything "more miserable." And as Tocqueville wrote much earlier in his *Voyage en Irlande* (1835), liberty "is, in truth, a holy thing," and the virtue that should inform it is nothing less than "the free choice of what is good." I am indebted to *L'abécédaire de Alexis de Tocqueville*, texts chosen by Françoise Mélonio and Charlotte Manzinni (Paris: Éditions de L'Observatoire, 2021) for drawing my attention to this passage and the one in the footnote that follows.

2 In an article cowritten with Gustave de Beaumont in *Le Commerce* dated November 24, 1844, Tocqueville dates his "politics" to 1789 and "not (17)92 or 1800." He thus explicitly repudiates Jacobin terror and Napoleonic despotism while reaffirming the largely aborted liberal promise of 1789. See Mélonio and Mazzini, *Ibid.*, pp. 213–214.

3 Joseph Epstein, *Alexis de Tocqueville: Democracy's Guide* (New York: Harper Perennial/Eminent Lives, 2007). All references to this volume will be cited internally and parenthetically in the text as *E* followed by the page number or numbers.

queville always remained something of a mystery even to himself. On the one hand, he was determined to leave his mark on the world through both his thought and his action, as I have already noted. He aspired to greatness and to fidelity to moral and political principles of the first order, including a profound and uncompromising commitment to political liberty. On the other hand, he suffered debilitating doubts about his capacity to make good on his hopes for himself and his country.

Epstein's little study, part of HarperCollins's "Eminent Lives" series, along with Hugh Brogan's massive biography *Alexis de Tocqueville: A Life*,[4] help us shed light on the mystery of Tocqueville. Brogan provides a plausible portrait of Tocqueville's world that includes many telling details, but his book, even though three times the length of Epstein's, fails to do justice to Tocqueville's political thought. By contrast, Epstein's short volume—part biographical sketch, part personal reflection—shows why Tocqueville *the thinker* remains to this day worthy of our attention and how Tocqueville's immense "powers of analysis and trenchancy of formulation" (*E*, 3) continue to move us well into the twenty-first century.

A Noble and Generous Soul

Brogan aptly depicts the royalist or "legitimist" circle that first shaped Tocqueville's heart and soul: a dignified and loving family tinged with sadness and tragedy; the deep and affecting friendships with Louis de Kergorlay, Gustave de Beaumont, "Francisque" Corcelle, Jean-Jacques Ampère, and many others that did so much to enrich his life and thought; and the drama of postrevo-

---

4 Hugh Brogan, *Alexis de Tocqueville: A Life* (New Haven, CN: Yale University Press, 2007). This book will henceforth be cited internally and parenthetically in the text as *B* followed by the page or page numbers.

lutionary France, afflicted by the revolutionary virus and unable to find for itself a stable, moderate, legitimate regime. This is the setting, artfully drawn, where Tocqueville's thought and action unfolded. Tocqueville's profound love of liberty and his noble and generous soul become, in Brogan's telling, almost palpable. We commune with the man and admire a greatness of soul that owes something to the dying world of aristocracy but isn't simply reducible to aristocratic convention.

This faithfulness to Tocqueville's world is all the more striking because Brogan himself shares so many of today's egalitarian prejudices. For him, democracy is an unqualified good, and anything that challenges it is evidence of aristocratic nostalgia, narrow class interest, or "masculinist ideology" (*B*, 277). (To his credit, Tocqueville did indeed defend the manly or "virile" virtues in a passionate but still measured way.) Brogan fails to take Tocqueville seriously as a political thinker who in some decisive respects transcended his milieu (*B*, 345–67). At the same time, Brogan fails to appreciate the broadest context of Tocqueville's life and thought, what Tocqueville called the great "democratic revolution" (as he called it in the "Author's Introduction" to *Democracy in America*) that was already radically transforming the Christian European world. Tocqueville's understanding of what might be gained and lost in the transition from the "aristocratic" to the "democratic" dispensation (great "orders of humanity" rather than regimes in the narrow sense of the term) gives Tocqueville's work a certain timeless intellectual and spiritual depth. That is why political philosophy, and not reductive cultural or intellectual history, is the best guide to study what endures in Tocqueville's political reflection and statesmanship.

Both Brogan and Epstein are sensitive to the traumatizing effects of the French Revolution on royalist France, not least on *la famille Tocqueville* (see especially *B*, 8-28). As Epstein puts it, "the revolution darkened Alexis' youth…and haunted all his mature years. Why the revolution had happened, what it wrought, and which precisely were its continuing effects on French life—these were to be among the main concerns behind all Tocqueville's writing" (*E*, 11). His mother, Louise Madeleine Le Peletier de Rosanbo de Tocqueville (1771–1836), was the granddaughter of the great Malesherbes, one of the most humane and liberal-minded figures of the final period of the Old Regime. Malesherbes was guillotined on April 23, 1794, after defending Louis XVI at his trial in the revolutionary Convention (*B*, 9–16). Many perished on both the Tocqueville and Rosanbo sides of the family. Tocqueville's parents escaped a similar fate only because of the timely overthrow of Robespierre's Terrorist regime on the ninth of Thermidor (July 27), 1794, in the revolutionary year 2 (1792, the year a new republican constitution was adopted in France, notoriously became "Year Zero"). Tocqueville's proud, disinterested love of liberty was a rare quality of a noble soul, but his lifelong disdain for the *esprit révolutionnaire* and his desire to extricate democracy from any entanglement with it were deeply rooted in personal experience. He was committed to severing any remaining links between democracy, rightly understood, and the revolutionary spirit of destruction and negation. He is the Burkean statesman but one operating "without transports of enthusiasm or of indignation" (the phrase is Raymond Aron's) amidst an irreversible democratic "revolution" that must be tempered rather than openly opposed.

As Brogan shows, Tocqueville's father, Hervé, was a model of the public-spirited aristocrat. A committed "Legitimist," attached through tradition and sentiment to the Bourbon family, he could not take the oath to the new "Orleanist" King Louis-Philippe, who was installed by the "bourgeois" revolution of July 1830 (*B*, 126).

As a result, he effectively retired from political life. But he had the good sense not to encourage Alexis to do so. His son believed that the Bourbon dynasty had forfeited, through political heavy-handedness and no small dose of stupidity, its right to govern France. But rather than immediately taking up a political career in the new regime, he set out for America and would soon begin to write the work that would make him famous.

With the publication of Volume 1 of *Democracy in America* in 1835, Tocqueville burst onto the stage as a thinker of the first order. He was only thirty years old. The most eminent men of his day rightly compared the book to Aristotle's *Politics* and Montesquieu's *Spirit of the Laws* (*B*, 285 and *E*, 98–99). That same year Tocqueville married Mary Mottley (he called her "Marie"), a bright, intense (and intermittently sickly) Englishwoman who was nine years his elder. This marriage to a middle-class English Protestant whom he respected and loved was a classic, even scandalous "misalliance," as Brogan points out. Their marriage was severely tested by Tocqueville's occasional infidelities—infidelities that he confessed and regretted—and by an emotional neediness on the part of both partners. For all their emotional ups and downs, however, Alexis and Mary were devoted to each other and remained the central figures in each other's lives to the end (see *B*, 99–101).

Though he could come across as haughty and cold to those who did not know him well, Tocqueville was capable of great devotion, which he extended not only to Marie but also to his inner circle of friends. Pride of place belongs to Gustave de Beaumont, whom he first met as a young lawyer at Versailles in the late 1820s. Epstein rightly states that the intense personal, political, and intellectual partnership between Tocqueville and Beaumont "is perhaps without an analogue in history." Their friendship was at least as significant as Marx and Engels's—and much more salutary. Tocqueville and Beaumont spoke with each other about everything, cowrote the impressive *Du Système pénitentiaire* (the study of prisons that was the official rationale for their trip to North America in the first place), wrote perfectly complementary works on American institutions and mores (*Democracy in America* and the insufficiently appreciated *Marie*, Beaumont's "novel" of race and slavery in America), and coordinated all their post-1830 political and intellectual activities. Theirs was a noble friendship Aristotle and Cicero would admire and approve of.

Democratic Justice and Human Greatness

If Brogan succeeds in recovering Tocqueville's world, however, he is woefully unsuccessful in capturing his thought. He censures the French political thinker for his deeply suspicious idea of "the tyranny of the majority," an idea that ostensibly reveals Tocqueville's insufficient confidence in "government of the people, by the people, and for the people" (*B*, 262–63). Brogan thus confuses democratic self-government with absolute popular sovereignty. He caricatures Tocqueville's measured analyses of the strengths and weaknesses of democracy as "the anxious degradation of American democracy." This biographer simply cannot distinguish between the candid friend, as Tocqueville calls himself in the brief Preface to Volume 2 of *Democracy in America*, and the indiscriminate flatterer of democracy, and he foolishly insists that all criticisms of democratic majoritarianism are proffered with anti-democratic intent.[5]

5 In the opening Preface to Volume 2 of *Democracy in America*, Tocqueville observes that he is "sincere" about the dangers that confront democracy precisely because he is not its "enemy." See Tocqueville, *Democracy in America*, Goldhammer edition, p. 479.

Similarly, Brogan cannot fathom that Tocqueville's equanimity in addressing the two great "anthropological forms" of political experience, democracy and aristocracy, is rooted in a profound thoughtfulness about both human nature and the nature of democracy. As Pierre Manent points out in a particularly insightful article ("Tocqueville, Political Philosopher" in the *Cambridge Companion to Tocqueville*), "these questions are currently resolved as follows: Tocqueville was a political man of old noble stock who made a resolute choice for democracy in his head while his heart remained filled with aristocratic 'nostalgia.'" Manent concedes that some of Tocqueville's own statements support such an interpretation. But a more penetrating reading suggests that Tocqueville's quasi-neutrality (at least on the philosophical plane) and equanimity between democracy and aristocracy are rooted in a fundamental tension in his own mind.

"On the one hand," Manent writes, there is

the perspective of justice. From this point of view, the modern, democratic conception of liberty—liberty as equal rights—is undoubtedly the just one. The ancient, aristocratic conception of liberty as privilege has to be given up. This judgment 'of the head' was also a judgment 'of the heart': Tocqueville, 'the Norman aristocrat,' shared the primary emotion of democracy when he spoke of men as 'obviously similar.'

Hence Tocqueville's hatred of racism and slavery, his profound admiration for America's political and constitutional arrangements, and his support for a political order that would bring "the people" into the political process in France. On the other hand, Manent continues, Tocqueville could never forget the perspective of grandeur, or independence, which he also calls liberty—but this is a liberty different from "equal liberty." Here the concern is no longer primarily with relations among men but with the quality of each man's soul, of his 'tone,' of his 'stature' or 'grandeur.' For Tocqueville, as for Aristotle, the perspective of 'magnanimity' does not coincide with that of 'justice,' and sometimes comes into contradiction with it.

By keeping this tension alive in our souls, Tocqueville succeeds in liberating us from democratic dogmatism and broadening our spiritual vision. Brogan understands none of this, alas, but Epstein shows a much fuller appreciation of the philosophical dimensions of Tocqueville's work. He recognizes that Tocqueville's endorsement of democracy is "somehow less than ebullient" (*E*, 92), but he knows that it is nonetheless wise and sincere.

Tocqueville despised the stultifying mediocrity of political life in France between 1830 and 1848. A political class led by the likes of François Guizot and Adolph Thiers, unimaginative and insensitive to new dangers on the horizon, did not stir his soul.[6] As we

6 At the same time, Tocqueville respected and even admired Guizot as a political historian and political philosopher. For nearly two years, he sat in on the public lectures that became *The History of Civilization in Europe* (1828), a work ably and eloquently translated by William Hazlitt in 1846 and republished by Penguin Books in 1997. As Larry Siedentop argues in his Introduction to the 1997 edition of this work, the young Tocqueville learned much from Guizot about the need to balance "central power and local autonomy." But without leaving his admiration for Guizot the thinker behind, Tocqueville believed that Guizot the statesman "betrayed [his own] decentralizing programme" by "using the bureaucratic structure of the French state to manipulate elections and subvert representative government" (Siedentop, Introduction, pp. xxxi–xxxiii). Guizot and Tocqueville both defended the ultimate "sovereignty of reason" or justice against claims of popular or democratic willfulness. But Tocqueville very much doubted Guizot's suggestion that democracy or liberalism would bow before the predominant "capacities" in the emerging representative political order and civil society. On this point, see the "Author's Introduction" to *Democracy in America* (Goldhammer translation), p. 6: "Does

shall see in the next section of this chapter, Tocqueville's struggle after February 1848 to defend a lawful republic against both the radical left and the Bonapartist right fired him with a renewed sense of purpose. It was at this point that he found his political faith of "liberty under God and the laws," a faith to which he gave eloquent expression in his 1856 masterpiece, *The Old Regime and the Revolution*.

The discerning reader of Tocqueville eventually confronts the mixture of magnanimity and anxiety ("restlessness" as he called it) that moved his noble soul. He was always haunted by doubt, which he described in 1831 as one of the three great "miseries" afflicting the human race (the others being death and illness). He lost his faith, at least in any truly orthodox or traditional form, at the age of sixteen, though he remained a broadly theistic thinker who repeatedly expressed confidence in the existence and Providence of God. In the political realm, he was more or less content with what he called "probabilistic" truths.[7] For example, one could not so much disprove various forms of historical and racial determinism as show their lack of plausibility—and their deeply pernicious effects on liberty and the human soul.

But in the philosophical and theological realms, Tocqueville

---

anyone think that democracy, having destroyed feudalism and vanquished kings, will be daunted by the bourgeois and the rich?" For Tocqueville, to ask the question was to answer it.

7 In a letter to Charles Stöffels from Philadelphia dated October 22, 1831, (see Alexis de Tocqueville, *Letters from America*, edited, translated, and with an Introduction by Frederick Brown (Yale University, Press, 2010, pp. 218–20)), Tocqueville rests content in most cases of moral and political judgment with reasonable "likelihoods, approximations" rather than "demonstrable truths." Such probabilistic truths protect one from excessive doubts that lead to debilitating "despair." Cicero makes a similar "probabilistic" argument at the service of avoiding the twin extremes of dogmatism and nihilistic skepticism. But Tocqueville is more visibly threatened by doubt that he links to disease and death as palpable evils that enervate the soul.

wanted to affirm something on the order of indubitable truth. He confessed and received communion before his death, partly to please his wife, Marie (a fervent convert to Catholicism), but also because he undoubtedly yearned to return to full communion with the Church of his youth. He was, in any case, as Brogan shows, only obliged to confess his sins and not to affirm his belief in all the dogmas of the Church (*B*, 625–26, 637–39). His ultimate religious convictions will always remain mysterious. The evidence suggests that he died with some of his doubts intact but with a renewed desire to find solace in the faith's great metaphysical and spiritual truths. Unusually confident in his principles and personal integrity, Tocqueville was yet never quite at home with himself or the world. One needs the help of both Aristotle's *Nicomachean Ethics* and Pascal's *Pensées* to account for his distinctive—and paradoxical—"greatness of soul."

A Mirror to Himself and Great Events: Tocqueville's Recollections

As I have emphasized, Tocqueville is the author of three great books: *Democracy in America*, *The Old Regime and the Revolution*, and the posthumously published *Recollections* of the French Revolution of 1848. The first two are best described as carefully crafted and philosophically astute guides to the "democratic revolution"[8] that was in the process of transforming the Western Christian world in the eighteenth and nineteenth centuries. As a statesman and political philosopher, Tocqueville hoped against hope that this revolution would culminate in a human and political order consistent with liberty and human dignity, doing justice to both

---

8 This "revolution" filled Tocqueville's soul with self-described "religious terror." See *Democracy in America*, Goldhammer translation, p. 6.

the equality of human beings and the "greatness" of man, which transcended the horizon of democratic equality. In these works, his rhetoric is measured and eloquent, carefully calibrated to the great task of defending human liberty and dignity in an age beset by new and troubling democratic discontents.

Recollections (*Souvenirs* in French) is the least known—and read—of these three works. This "absolutely thrilling" book, as Raymond Aron called it, gives us unique access to Tocqueville the human being and thinker. It is deeply personal without ever being self-indulgent. Tocqueville wrote it for the drawer, or rather for posthumous publication. It only appeared (in an expurgated form) in 1893, thirty-four years after Tocqueville's death, and a complete edition had to wait until 1942 for publication. Its best translator, Arthur Goldhammer, expertly captures Tocqueville's style in this work, at once aphoristic and eminently quotable and also deeply discerning about men and events.[9] He captures Tocqueville's lucidity and eloquence, as he had already done in his previous translations of *Democracy in America* and *The Old Regime*. This is no mean achievement.

Tocqueville's utter frankness in *Recollections* sets it apart from his better-known works. He claims, a bit deceptively, that he wrote "for himself alone" as a "mirror in which I shall enjoy looking at myself and my contemporaries, not a painting intended for public viewing." But the book is so deftly written and is such a great work of political literature that one must doubt Tocqueville's claim that he wrote it merely as a "solitary pleasure." Its readership was the next generation or two (and those who followed) or anyone who

---

9 See Alexis de Tocqueville, *Recollections: The French Revolution of 1848 and Its Aftermath*, edited by Olivier Zunz, translated by Arthur Goldhammer (Charlottesville, VA: University of Virginia Press, 2016). All subsequent citations will appear internally and parenthetically in the text as *R* followed by the appropriate page number or numbers.

would turn again to Tocqueville for a "true portrait of human society" and the "virtues and vices" (*S*, 3) of his contemporaries and the Revolution, French and democratic, that never seemed to come to a satisfactory conclusion.

The book begins with a portrait of the Orléanist monarchy, headed by King Louis-Philippe, that dominated France from the Revolution of 1830 until the Revolution of 1848. As I mentioned at the opening of this chapter, Tocqueville was a parliamentarian who was actively engaged in the political life of this semi-liberal monarchy. As I have noted, he found the regime to be tolerably free but corrupted by an oligarchic spirit marked by an excessive and degrading taste for material well-being. It was bourgeois but without the elevation that comes when the middle class opens itself to the aristocracy above and the people below (*S*, 4). Louis-Philippe was that irony of ironies: a bourgeois king, mediocre but not particularly oppressive. Reasonably free, Orléanist France was ruled by a "government without virtue and greatness" (*S*, 4), as Tocqueville put it in the opening chapter of *Recollections*. In decisive respects, Tocqueville found the rule of this bourgeois king and his historian–Prime Minister François Guizot to be stifling of authentic initiatives and a vibrant political life: "what was most lacking, especially at the end, was political life itself" (*S*, 8). Tocqueville was no enemy of constitutional monarchy—he even believed it to be the best available regime for the French—but he wanted to see an opening of the political sphere to the full energies of society. He was firmly convinced that the status quo could not hold, and he even predicted the Revolution of 1848 in a speech to the National Assembly several weeks before its outbreak (see the excerpt from that speech in *S*, 11). One might have thought that Tocqueville would welcome the demise of a political order he thought too oligarchic and found too stifling. But Tocqueville was too sober to rejoice in yet another reckless instantiation of the never-ending French Revolution. He fully appreciated that revolution rarely gave rise to what he called "a moderate, regulated liberty disciplined by faith, mores, and laws" (*S*, 47). This had been his "sacred project" for twenty years, and the French Revolution of 1848 set it back yet another generation or two. His reaction to the Revolution was thus despondency and the growing conviction that the French were destined to move endlessly back and forth from "license" to "oppression" (*S*, 47), never finding the *juste milieu* or a democracy worthy of the name. This disruptive revolution never seemed to approach an end. Tocqueville feared that the French were destined to "ply the seas forever" (*S*, 48).

Tocqueville provides a remarkably vivid account of the Revolution itself. He was appalled by the tendency of almost every current of French society to imitate the actors from the original French Revolution, as if the Revolution itself was an exercise in theatrical display. In a dramatic exchange, he told his dear friend Ampère, whom he found too enamored of a revolution that could only undermine ordered liberty, that he, like the French people as a whole, was addicted to "literary politics." The "literary spirit in politics" prefers "what is ingenious and new rather than what is true, what makes an interesting scene rather than what serves a useful purpose...It is responding to the talent and elocution of the actors rather than to the consequences of the play" (*S*, 48). Rarely has the French propensity over the last two centuries toward political irresponsibility and bouts of revolutionary inebriation been better described. As Raymond Aron noted sixty years ago, the euphoria of Ampère better describes the reaction of French intellectuals to revolutionary eruptions (think May 1968) than the sobriety of a Tocqueville (or Aron himself). Too many intellectuals think of revolution in theatrical or even eschatological terms, as something that will lead to vaguely defined human "emancipation." Tocqueville's *Recollections* continue to provide a powerful antidote to this revolutionary illusion that appears to be a permanent temptation in late modernity.

General and Particular Causes

In the tradition of his great predecessor Montesquieu, Tocqueville tries to do justice to both the "general" and "particular" causes that led to France's latest, and in his view unwelcome, revolutionary conflagration. In a beautiful formulation, he pronounces his hatred of "absolute systems that see all historical events as dependent on grand first causes linked together in ineluctable sequence, thus banishing individual human beings from the history of the human race" (*S*, 45). That is not Tocqueville's way. His explanation of the causes of the French Revolution of 1848 does justice to the full range of the "general causes" that prepared the way for the Revolution (from the Industrial Revolution and new socialist doctrines to the centralization of the state that "reduced the work of revolution to seizing Paris and its ready-made machinery of government") to those particular causes, including a "maladroit" and irresponsible opposition to the "senile imbecility" of Louis-Philippe on the eve of the Revolution (*S*, 45-46). Tocqueville is a forceful and convincing critic of "democratic historians" (as he called them in Volume 2 of *Democracy in America*) who succumb to historical determinism and are too lazy or incompetent to chronicle the role that freely choosing individuals play in the unfolding of historical events both great and small. This is one of Tocqueville's enduring philosophical contributions and a useful corrective to the tendency of radically modern doctrines to efface the human element altogether (Marxism, deconstruction, social history, neuroscience, and myriad other intellectual currents come to mind). For Tocqueville, the freely acting moral and political agent cannot be reduced to things other than himself. Human beings are not playthings of historical, sociological, or biological forces without any capacity to shape events for good or ill.[10]

Socialist Servitude and Bonapartist Authoritarianism

Recollections reveals socialism as Tocqueville's great bête noire during the Revolution of 1848. The socialists wanted nothing less than to attack and replace the "fundamental laws" (*S*, 54–55) of society, including private property and the family. At one point, he speculates that societies are more malleable than he and other defenders of order typically acknowledge (*S*, 55). Perhaps the socialists might succeed in establishing a society of a radically new kind. But that society would not accord with liberty and human dignity. In a beautiful and discerning speech from September 12, 1848, ("The Speech on the Right to Work") that is included among the impressive ancillary documents in the Goldhammer edition of *Recollections* (*S*, 235–41), Tocqueville attacks socialism for its "persistent, strenuous, and immoderate appeal to man's material passions" (seen in the revolutionary unleashing of massive greed and envy on the part of the poorer classes) and its "unrelenting" assault on "the very principle of individual property" (*S*, 236). He also lambasted the socialists for their "pro-

---

10 See the final words of the second volume of *Democracy in America* (p. 834 in the Goldhammer edition): "It is beyond the ability of nations today to prevent conditions from becoming equal; but it is within their power to decide whether equality will lead them into servitude or liberty, enlightenment or barbarism, prosperity or misery."

In the previous paragraph, Tocqueville famously upholds a vast realm of freedom and agency within the "fatal circle" that is democratic modernity. That paradoxical affirmation of freedom within circumscribed limits is at the heart of Tocqueville's political reflection and political moderation.

found distrust" of "liberty" and "human reason" (*S*, 237). He, for one, saw socialism as at best the road to a "schoolmaster" state (we today would say "nanny state") and at worst a new road to servitude (*S*, 237–38). Tocqueville was in no way an opponent of public charity to relieve the plight of the poor, but he was convinced that socialism would bring ruin to every stratum of society even as it destroyed the fundamental laws on which society is based. No one can reasonably accuse Tocqueville of opposing socialism in the name of oligarchy or the selfishness of the privileged classes. He wanted to relieve the plight of the poor without creating a new and deadly despotism and a retrenchment of the human spirit and its capacity for great and noble deeds. About that Tocqueville was surely right.

I would be remiss if I did not give examples of Tocqueville's tremendous gift of literary portraiture. His account in *Recollections* of a lunch discussion with the writer George Sand on the eve of the socialist "June Days," when Paris's workers rose up in rebellion against the new republic, is a particular gem. Sand was a well-informed and spirited partisan of the revolutionary workers, and she eerily describes the terrible fate of Paris's bourgeois (and other defenders of "order") if conflict were to break out. Tocqueville paints this scene deftly and with an air of foreboding (*S*, 95–96). He also mocks his own inability to remember the names and faces of the mediocrities who surround him in democratic politics (*S*, 59). While too decent to disdain them, he cannot recall them very well. And in a splendid diptych, he contrasts his unnamed drunken porter, "a socialist by temperament," who threatened in a local bar room to kill him when he got home (he did not deliver on the promise), with his valet Eugène, who possessed the self-control and temperament of a philosopher and who was loyal to Tocqueville and fought to defend the Republic (*S*, 112). These sketches are both artful and instructive and help make *Recollections* an impressively gripping work of literature in its own right.

In his helpful introduction to the Goldhammer volume, the historian Olivier Zunz comments on Tocqueville's "rejuvenation" (*S*, xviii) when he began to take part in the electoral politics of the Second Republic. Tocqueville ran a dignified campaign and committed himself once more to his program of "liberty and human dignity." He was determined to "defeat demagogy with democracy" (*S*, 77), perhaps the best short description of his noble *political* project. "Never had a goal seemed nobler or clearer to [him]" (*S*, 77). But events intervened with the election of Louis-Napoléon as president of the Second Republic. As his foreign minister for five months, Tocqueville tried to rein him in. Eventually, Louis-Napoléon established a "bastard monarchy" (*S*, 144), as Tocqueville so suggestively called it, after the prince-president staged a *coup d'état* in December 1851. Tocqueville vehemently opposed the socialism opened up by the Revolution of 1848. But he could not countenance for a minute an authoritarian dictatorship (at once conservative and modernist-progressive) that abandoned political liberty in order to obtain social stability. This conservative-minded liberal was a party of one, rejecting both the perils of socialist servitude and the temptation of conservative authoritarianism. In *Recollections*, we see him at work, loyal to his principles, and committed to a future wherein liberty and a modicum of greatness might coexist.

Recollections is essential reading for all who want to understand modern revolution as well as to appreciate the perspicacious eye, human greatness, and inimitable pen of Alexis de Tocqueville. Socialist revolution and the accompanying if opposed reactionary flight from free politics knew no more discerning and determined opponent. In Tocqueville's heart and mind, in his thought and action, the best of classical conservatism and classical liberalism come together, much as they did for Burke. But unlike Burke, a statesman and thinker whom Tocqueville both criticized and admired, Tocqueville saw no hope of rescuing even the slightest residues of the European Old Regime.[11]

Appendix: Tocqueville on Race and Slavery

Let us conclude this chapter by examining Tocqueville's views on slavery in America with the help of the indispensable *Tocqueville on America after 1840: Letters and Other Writings,* edited and translated by Aurelian Craiutu and Jeremy Jennings.[12]

Tocqueville on America after 1840 is a remarkable volume that includes *everything* the French political thinker and statesman wrote on the United States or American-related themes after the publication of the second volume of *Democracy in America* in 1840 until his death in 1859. Most of the material previously appeared in French in the authoritative version of his *Oeuvres complètes*, but the vast majority is available in English for the first time, and even some of the handwritten letters to Tocqueville from his American interlocutors were transcribed for this volume. It is thus a treasure trove for students of Tocqueville and American democracy.

The editors' thirty-nine-page interpretive essay (accompanied

11 For Tocqueville, Burke failed to appreciate that the old constitution of France, its lauded "ancient liberties," were for all intents and purposes moribund and beyond resuscitation well before 1789. The Estates General, for example, had not met since 1614 until it was called back into existence in 1788. But the mind of Burke, whose greatness and nobility Tocqueville readily acknowledged, was greatly "sharpened by the loathing that the Revolution inspired in him from its inception." See Tocqueville, *The Ancien Régime and the Revolution* (Goldhammer-Elster edition), pp. 27 and 12 (in that order).

12 See Aurelian Craiutu and Jeremy Jennings editors, *Tocqueville on America after 1840: Letters and Other Writings* (Cambridge, UK, and New York, New York, 2006). Hereafter cited parenthetically as *T1840* followed by page numbers.

by fourteen small-print pages of notes) is an invaluable guide to Tocqueville's engagement with America over a thirty-year period, from his nine-month trip with Gustave de Beaumont to the United States in 1831–32 until his renewed attentiveness to things American in the final decade of his life. The editors accurately convey Tocqueville's disenchantment with the broad direction of American democracy in the 1850s. But the letters, speeches, and writings they compiled do not show their author radically departing from his analysis in *Democracy*. To begin with, as the editors acknowledge, Tocqueville's growing pessimism during the 1850s had as much to do with the erosion of liberty in France during Napoleon III's quasi-despotic reign as it did with his renewed attention to America. What's more, Tocqueville was never quite as "optimistic" about democracy, even American democracy, as Craiutu and Jennings sometimes suggest. To be sure, the French political thinker placed considerable hopes in the "great experiment of Self Government that is currently taking place in America" (*T1840*, 224), as he put it in a letter to Edward Vernon Childe in 1857. This experiment elevated democracy and was inseparable from its moral promise. Its failure, he told Childe, would "be the end of political liberty on earth" (*T1840*, 224). There is no evidence, however, that Tocqueville ever *despaired* about America and her prospects or even came close to doing so. One can grant that a hypothetical third volume of *Democracy* might have gone further in emphasizing peril rather than promise, but the evils of democratic despotism, the possibility of unprecedented democratic forms of human degradation, and heartfelt warnings about the incompatibility of slavery with Christian morality and democratic self-government were already essential themes of the first two volumes of *Democracy in America*.

Today, certain liberal political theorists have made something of a cottage industry out of trying to discredit Tocqueville because of his alleged fondness for imperialism. This may culminate, and soon, in an effort to "cancel" him (the contemporary assault on human and political greatness knows no bounds). It is true that he was not opposed in principle to imperialism, whether that of the British in India or the French in Algeria, though he could be extremely critical of colonial abuses in both countries, as Churchill was later. Tocqueville was open to the "greatness" of a humane, civilizing empire, which could act as a corrective, however problematic, to bourgeois democracy's individualist, materialist preoccupations. But he was adamantly opposed to slavery and in 1839 sponsored a bill in the Chamber of Deputies for its abolition in the French colonies. Tocqueville's letters to his American friends express serious reservations about colonialism *as an end in itself* and ought to give pause to those "postcolonial" theorists committed to dismissing him as a single-minded partisan of imperial domination. In a letter to Jared Sparks dated December 11, 1852, Tocqueville argued that America "has nothing to fear but from itself, from the excesses of democracy, the spirit of adventure and conquest, the sentiment of and the excessive pride in its strength, and the passions of youth." He counseled "moderation," which he insisted was needed in nations "no less than individuals" (*T1840*, 139). In other letters, he expressed his concern that Americans were in the process of becoming like Hobbes's *puer robustus*, "robust children" who lacked the moderation and maturity to exercise their power in a responsible way (*T1840*, 183, 336). Tocqueville was no advocate of an immoral "power politics."

Tocqueville's letters from this period suggest a series of related concerns that together reinforced his anxiety about the future of American democracy. He worried, and in retrospect inordinately so, about the massive influx of German immigrants to the United States (*T1840*, 188). In his view they lacked the habits of self-government necessary to sustain liberty. He was also profoundly worried about what he perceived as a decline in American mores. He was convinced that the "spirit of adventurism" was dramatically at odds with the sound, sturdy character and respect for law he had heralded in *Democracy in America*, especially in Volume 1. He lamented, too, the absence of real statesmen on the American scene and wondered if the sober common sense of the American people was enough to avoid impending disaster. These worries are as relevant as ever.

Yet all of these concerns pale beside his greatest preoccupation during this period: the threat that the expansion of slavery posed to America's moral integrity, self-respect, and international prestige. For the most part, Tocqueville scholars (Craiutu and Jennings included) haven't noticed that their subject's positions on union, liberty, abolitionism, and the expansion of slavery are in decisive respects the same as Abraham Lincoln's (though there is no evidence that the Frenchman ever commented on him even though they were roughly contemporaries). Tocqueville articulates essentially Lincolnian judgments about these matters without ever appealing to Lincoln's "glorious" Declaration of Independence. What accounts for this remarkable convergence between the sympathetic French commentator on America's unfolding tragedy and the statesman-poet who would so eloquently summon Americans back to the "better angels of our nature"?

For Tocqueville and Lincoln, the heart of the matter was the same: the repeal of the Missouri Compromise of 1820 and the extension of slavery to new states and territories entailed a betrayal of America's moral promise. Both men affirmed blacks' humanity and intrinsic dignity. Both used their considerable

intellectual and rhetorical powers to attack the dangerous con-
flation of self-government with the right to own and trade in
human beings. But principle needed to be guided by prudence.
Tocqueville, like Lincoln, was opposed to the abolitionists "as far
as that party wanted to bring forth the premature and dangerous abolition of slavery in those districts where this abominable
institution has always existed." (These are Tocqueville's words,
not Lincoln's, although a reader would be forgiven for confusing
them.) He considered the spread of this "horrible plague onto a
large portion of the earth which has been free from it until now"
to be nothing less than a "crime against mankind," one that was
"both dreadful and unpardonable" (all quotations in this paragraph are from *T1840*, 224).

In another letter, Tocqueville expressed himself in similar terms:
"the extension of this horrible evil beyond the already too extensive limits within which it is confined" was "one of the greatest
crimes that human beings could commit against the general cause
of humanity." It filled him, a fifty-year-old Frenchman who had
"seen four or five revolutions," with "powerful political passions"
(*T1840*, 195). The same might be said of Lincoln, who came out
of political retirement with his 1854 Peoria speech, assailing the
Kansas-Nebraska Act in order to recall Americans to "our ancient
faith" (a speech to be examined in our next chapter). This faith
did not demand slavery's immediate abolition, but it did require
vigorous opposition to its expansion as well as a renewed commitment to the bedrock truth that "all men are created equal."

In the Peoria speech, Lincoln appealed to a "moral sense" argument by criticizing the reduction of some human beings to the
status of animals, the equivalent of "wild horses, wild buffaloes,
or wild bears." He pointed out that Americans had outlawed the
slave trade in 1820 on punishment of death; they did "not so treat

the man who deals in corn, cattle, or tobacco." What Stephen A. Douglas liked to call "the sacred right of self-government" could not include, Lincoln argued, the right to "govern another man *without that other's consent*." To do so would violate the moral law as well as that "sheet anchor of American republicanism, Our Declaration of Independence." Of course, everything stood or fell with the recognition of blacks' humanity, a recognition that Lincoln argued was grudgingly acknowledged even by the partisans of slavery when they and their children shunned those who traded in slaves.

Tocqueville's own case against slavery closely resembled Lincoln's. In 1855, at the request of the abolitionist Maria Weston Chapman, he composed a short, eloquent, and moving "Testimony Against Slavery" that appeared the following year in the antislavery journal *The Liberty Bell* (T1840, all the quotes to follow from 169). As a "persevering enemy of despotism everywhere" and "an old and sincere friend of America," Tocqueville expressed his chagrin that "the freest people in the world is, at the present time, almost the only one among civilized and Christian nations which yet maintains personal servitude." He was "uneasy" at "seeing Slavery retard her progress, tarnish her glory, furnish arms to her detractors, compromise the future career of the Union." He went on to speak about being "moved at the spectacle of man's degradation by man." Without explicitly appealing to either the Declaration of Independence or the Constitution, he expressed his "hope" that he will "see the day when the law will grant equal civil liberty to all the inhabitants of the same empire, as God accords the freedom of the will, without distinction, to the dwellers upon earth." The call to "equal civil liberty" anticipated Lincoln's own noble call for "a new birth of freedom" in the Gettysburg Address of 1863.

Tocqueville appealed to the decency, self-respect, and honor of a free, Christian, self-governing people. A free people cannot be a slave-owning people without compromising its soul or risking the loss of its liberty. Tocqueville's "silence," or near silence, about the Declaration in both *Democracy in America* and in his later writings and letters about America has nothing to do with neglect for the affirmation of "common humanity" that undergirds it. As a Frenchman who had lived through the ravages of the French Revolution (and of subsequent French revolutions that appealed to its authority), Tocqueville had an understandable suspicion of "abstract" appeals to the "rights of man." In Europe, they had been used to undermine traditions and institutions that were necessary to the continuity of civilization and the moral foundations of representative government. In *Democracy in America*, with the French context ever in mind, Tocqueville emphasized the Americans' Puritan "point of departure." However "barbarous" some of their laws were, the Puritans managed to successfully weave together the "spirit of liberty" and the "spirit of religion." And without losing sight of the great truth that "all men are created equal," Tocqueville emphasized the U.S. Constitution as a supreme act of moral and political prudence. It is a mistake to consult Tocqueville for an exhaustive account of the American founding. That was never his paramount concern. Rather, we should turn to him for an unusually discerning account of American institutions and mores and for a penetrating description of the effects—all the effects—of modernity's unrelenting "democratic revolution." The Norman aristocrat fully deserves his self-characterization as "half an American citizen" (*T1840*, 136). His adamant opposition to the persistence of slavery in a foreign land he loved was rooted in fidelity to the cause of self-government, in abiding commitment to liberty and human dignity, and in an ultimate confidence in what Lincoln so memorably called in 1861 "the better angels of our nature."

Sources and Suggested Readings

The place to begin with Tocqueville are his three indisputable masterworks: *Democracy in America*, translated by Arthur Gold-hammer (New York: Library of America, 2004); *The Ancien Régime and the French Revolution*, edited by Jon Elster, translated by Arthur Goldhammer (New York, New York: Cambridge University Press, 2011); and *Recollections: The French Revolution of 1848 and Its Aftermath*, edited by Olivier Zunz, translated by Arthur Goldhammer (Charlottesville, VA: University of Virginia Press, 2016). I have also consulted the fine but more literal translation by Harvey C. Mansfield and Delba Winthrop published by the University of Chicago Press in 2000.

The first opening epigraph is drawn from *Democracy in America* (the Goldhammer translation), p.17.

The second epigraph comes from the final pages of Tocqueville's "Foreword" to *The Ancien Régime and the French Revolution* (Goldhammer translation), p. 6.

Besides the biographical portraits by Brogan and Epstein, I recommend the detailed and authoritative work by André Jardin, *Tocqueville: A Biography*, published in translation by Farrar, Straus and Giroux in 1988.

Tocqueville's revealing letter to Louis de Kergorlay dated December 15, 1850, can be found in *Alexis de Tocqueville: Selected Letters on Politics and Society*, edited by Roger Boesche, translated by James Toupin and Roger Boesche (Berkeley, CA: University of California Press, 1985), pp. 252–58.

On Tocqueville's marked preference for "1789" over everything

Robespierre and Napoleon represent, see the Foreword to *The Ancien Régime and the French Revolution*, p. 4.

On Tocqueville's acceptance of democracy "without transports of enthusiasm or of indignation," see Aron, *Main Currents in Sociological Thought: Volume 1: Montesquieu, Comte, Marx, Tocqueville, and the Sociologists and the Revolution of 1848* (Oxford, UK: Routledge Classics, 2019), p. 272. For the "absolutely thrilling" character of *Recollections*, see Aron, p. 255. For the remarkably cheerful attitude of contemporary intellectuals toward revolution, see Aron, p. 256.

Pierre Manent's luminous essay "Tocqueville: Political Philosopher" can be found in *The Cambridge Companion to Tocqueville,* edited by Cheryl B. Welch (Cambridge, UK: Cambridge University Press, 2006), pp. 108–20. I have quoted from pp. 116–17. There are many other fine essays in this volume.

I am indebted to Harvey C. Mansfield's lucid and insightful discussion of *Recollections* in his sprightly volume *Tocqueville: A Very Short Introduction* (Oxford, UK: Oxford University Press, 2010), Chapter 6, pp. 102–14.

See Volume 2, Part I, Chapter 20 of *Democracy of America* for Tocqueville's powerful dissection of the fatalism and determinism beloved by historians in a democratic age. See the Goldhammer translation, pp. 569–73.

For any considered judgment on Tocqueville's final verdict on American democracy, it is necessary to consult *Tocqueville on America After 1840: Letters and Other Writings*, edited and translated by Aurelian Craiutu and Jeremy Jennings (Cambridge, UK: Cambridge University Press, 2009).

On the Pascalian dimensions of Tocqueville's thought and soul, I am indebted to numerous writings by the late Peter Augustine Lawler. Tocqueville never stopped thinking about "the greatness and misery of man," especially as it was effected by the unfolding "democratic revolution," a revolution that filled him with both hope and "religious terror."

There is no doubt Lincoln was a politician—has anyone ever seriously thought otherwise? Lincoln and Millard Fillmore were both politicians, but what does this term tell us about them? But if the word politician *says little about Lincoln, the term* statesman *tells us more.*

—STEVEN B. SMITH,
Introduction to *The Writings of Abraham Lincoln*
(Yale University Press, 2012)

It is said an Eastern monarch once charged his wise men to invent him a sentence, to be ever in view, and which should be true and appropriate in all times and situations. They presented him the words: "And this, too, shall pass away." How much it expresses! How chastening in the hour of pride!—how consoling in the depths of affliction! "And this, too, shall pass away." And yet let us hope it is not quite *true. Let us hope, rather, that by the best cultivation of the physical world, beneath and around us; and the intellectual and moral world within us, we shall secure an individual, social, and political prosperity and happiness, whose course shall be onward and upward, and which, while the earth endures, shall not pass away.*

—ABRAHAM LINCOLN,
"Address to the Wisconsin State Agricultural Society,"
Milwaukee, Wisconsin, September 30, 1859, in
The Writings of Abraham Lincoln

5

ABRAHAM LINCOLN:
TOUCHED BY PRUDENCE AND
GRACE TO COMPLETE THE
PROMISE OF AMERICA

Democratic peoples are prone to impatience and ingratitude in the best of circumstances. But in a highly ideologized climate marked by collective self-loathing and an unremitting desire to repudiate the inheritance of the past, ingratitude becomes inseparable from a vulgar and destructive nihilism. George Washington sacrificed a great deal to help establish a regime of liberty, and he subordinated narrow personal ambition to an austere sense of public duty and reputation well earned. He was truly the father of his country. But in the emerging dispensation that is replacing our old constitutional order, the fact that he owned slaves must negate everything else, come what may. A tyrannical "presentism," as George F. Will has called it, drives out both patriotic attachment and a capacity for measured judgment and admiration. Washington's undoubted greatness of soul, his noble and prudent leadership in times of war and peace, and his unflagging commitment to the cause of free, constitutional government, is dismissed in one fell swoop as the vanguards of political correctness succumb to a moralistic rage that owes little or nothing to authentic moral and political judgment. The fact that Washington opposed slavery in principle and did nothing to promote and expand it counts for nothing. The fact that our first president freed his slaves in his final will and testament (an admirable act at once private and public) and provided for their education and economic sustenance for years to come is surely unknown by the progressive school boards and activists who wish to erase Washington's name from every school and building in the nation he did so much to establish and sustain.[1] In truth, those who wish to purge him from our history know nothing about Washington or his greatness, an ignorance that feeds their desire to cancel him once and for all.

Their nihilism can be constrasted with the unstinting admiration that another great president had for Washington, the father of an experiment in self-government that, for all its flaws, was rooted in an "abstract truth, applicable to all men at all times": the truth that "all men are created equal" (Letter to Henry L. Pierce and Others, April 6, 1859 in *TWAL*, 243–44). The President I am referring to, Abraham Lincoln, never lost sight of the "apple of gold," the affirmation of equality under God, that informed our constitutional "frame of silver" ("Fragment on the Constitution and the Union," c. January 1861, *TWAL*, 321–22). In making this point, Lincoln brilliantly draws upon Proverbs 25. The founders, he argued repeatedly and persuasively, most notably in his Cooper Union Address of February 27, 1860, made only one concession to slavery, the one rooted in "necessity," as Lincoln called it (*TWAL*, 283–95). They could not abolish slavery where it already existed without preventing the establishment of "a more perfect Union" in the first place. But they did what they could: denouncing this morally repugnant institution, forbidding

---

1 See "Last Will and Testament" (July 9, 1799) in *Washington: Writings*, John Rhodechamel, editor (New York: Library of America, 1997), pp. 1022–42.

its expansion to the Northwest Territories in 1787 with the so-called Northwest Ordinance (largely designed and promoted by Thomas Jefferson), and allowing for the outlawing of the inhuman slave trade in 1808. In addition, these conscientious men refused to sully the Constitution of 1787, a "glorious freedom document"[2] as Frederick Douglass rightly called it in a memorable speech in 1852, by including any direct reference to slaves or slavery in the language of the Constitution. Imperfectly and haphazardly, the founders attempted to put slavery "on the road to eventual extinction" (*TWAL*, 82–85).

Coming for Lincoln

Abraham Lincoln, the greatest of our presidents and surely the most philosophically minded, would complete the founders' work by saving a union dedicated to the great proposition of liberty and equality "under God," defeating a Confederate rebellion dedicated to the indefinite perpetuation of chattel slavery, freeing the slaves, and pointing toward "a new birth of freedom" (*TWAL*, 417) that would redeem the promise of the American founding and vindicate what he called "the last best hope on earth."

Now the cancelers have come for Lincoln too. His statues have been toppled, and his character has been slandered by those who specialize in slogans, half-truths, and tiresome ideological clichés. Once again, the ignorance of the ideologues is palpable. This humane, generous man who truly "loathed slavery"[3] (in Frederick

---

2 See Frederick Douglass, "What is the Slave to the Fourth of July?," July 5, 1852, in *The Speeches of Frederick Douglass: A Critical Edition*, edited by John R. McKivigan, Julie Husband, and Heather L. Kaufman (New Haven, CT: Yale University Press, 2018, pp. 55–92), especially pp. 88–90.

3 Douglass, "The Freedman's Monument to Abraham Lincoln" (April 14, 1876) in *Ibid.*, pp. 337–55, especially p. 351. "He loathed and hated slavery." Douglass writes about Lincoln with the requisite passion and just the right emphases.

Douglass's words) is denounced as a racist largely on the basis of quotations taken out of context or read without the slightest degree of imagination or generosity. A new generation of historians tells us that the slaves freed themselves and that Lincoln had little or nothing to do with it. And on the paleoconservative right, the high political prudence of Lincoln is often confused with Jacobinism, political messianism, and radical egalitarianism, one claim more unmeasured and absurd than the other. Madness meets stupidity and ingratitude in a way that ought to shame the American people.

A Conservatism of Definition

In truth, Lincoln's noble fidelity to the founders and his concomitant effort to remind Americans of the transcendental ground of human freedom both complete and elevate the work of the founders. Richard Weaver was right in *The Ethics of Rhetoric* (1953) to discern in Lincoln a humane conservatism rooted in what Weaver called "the argument from definition." Lincoln, an avid student of Euclid, made excellent use of definitions and distinctions. Like a true conservative, Weaver unforgettably argues, he saw "the universe as a paradigm of essences, of which the phenomenology of the world is a sort of continuing approximation." His conservatism of definition (which was perfectly compatible with classical liberal political economy and Whig constitutionalism, as we shall see) had no place for the inhuman sophistry that confused a black man or woman with mere chattel to be used at the sufferance of an owner's cruelty and selfishness. Lincoln made clear that the equality of free men and women had nothing to do with equality in talent, intelligence, moral character, or any other number of human attributes, let alone which end of a gun their ancestors found themselves on. They were equal in their right to self-governance and to keep what they had earned "by the sweat of their brow." Lincoln saw undoubted nobility in the moral axioms set forth in the Declaration of Independence. Weaver quotes an exemplary passage of Lincoln's on the founders' intent in that document: "They meant to set up a standard maxim for free society, which should be familiar to all, and revered by all; constantly looked to, constantly labored for, and even though never perfectly attained, constantly approximated, and thereby constantly spreading and deepening its influence and augmenting the happiness and value of life to all people of all colors everywhere." Note well: "People of all colors everywhere." Blacks are by no means excluded from the promise of the Declaration, contrary to the egregious thinking of both Senator Stephen Douglas in the Lincoln-Douglas debates and of Chief Justice Roger Taney in the egregious Dred Scott decision of 1857 (see Lincoln, "Speech on the Dred Scott Decision," at Springfield, Illinois, June 26, 1857, in *TWAL*, 108–19).

Weaver, like later students of Lincoln's thought and statecraft such as Joseph G. Fornieri and Allen C. Guelzo, sees in Lincoln a profound and morally serious capacity to conjugate principle and prudence without succumbing either to unprincipled pragmatism or moral preening and virtue signaling, as we say today. He opposed slavery with every bone in his body but saw that the Abolitionists dangerously eschewed prudence by falsely rejecting the Constitution and its principled compromises as "the Devil's work." By thus undermining the moral foundation of the union, they made it much more likely that slavery would be endlessly perpetuated if the slave-owning states chose to go their separate way, as they would indeed do in 1861. Theirs was a self-righteous "ethics of intention," in Max Weber's famous words, emphasizing conviction at the expense of political responsibility. And yet they, and not Lincoln, are considered the true heroes today (although some among the "woke" take aim at their alleged "whiteness" too). This cultural revolution, like all ideological revolutions, very quickly devours its children—and former heroes. No one is safe from moralistic—and nihilistic—rage. Lincoln's great and capacious soul responded to the requirements of righteousness but never succumbed to moral rage.

But Weaver thoughtfully adds that Lincoln was no tepid "middle-of-the-roader." He did not so much seek the middle ground as attempt to promote "reform according to law; that is according to definition." Lincoln, like Burke, admirably and successfully combined conservatism and reform even if Burke's "circumstantial" conservatism was hardly a "conservatism of definition." Yet, however paradoxically, both Burke and Lincoln were practitioners and adherents of a politics of prudence, as Greg Weiner persuasively argues in his recent book *Old Whigs: Burke, Lincoln, and the Politics of Prudence.* In that regard, Abraham Lincoln is no more a Jacobin than Edmund Burke, the great nemesis of Jacobin fanaticism rooted in the spirit of cruel and coercive abstractions. Lincoln knew human nature and human right, its limits and possibilities; the Jacobins decidedly did not.

Lincoln and Honorable Ambition

Robert Faulkner aptly described Lincoln as a classic representative of "honorable ambition" at work in the political realm. His old law partner in Springfield, Illinois, William Herndon, who knew him well, went so far as to describe his ambition as "a little engine that knew no rest." But contrary to the speculations of the literary critic and man of letters Edmund Wilson in his once famous 1939 book *Patriotic Gore,* Lincoln did not identify himself with those whom he described in his January 27, 1838, Lyceum Address as belonging "to the family of the lion, and the tribe of the eagle" (*TWAL*, 12), spiritual heirs of an Alexander, a Caesar, or a Napoleon. He warned against the rise of lawlessness that will give "towering genius [that] disdains a beaten path" (*TWAL*, 12) its long-awaited opportunity to subvert free government since decent people are sure to lose their attachment to free government. In the conclusion of that speech, Lincoln recommends a "political religion" of law-abidingness rooted in "sober reason" (*TWAL*, 14) and a deep fidelity to the project of self-government bequeathed by Washington, among others, to stand in place of the revolutionary passions that Americans used to be able to count on, with enmity then directed at the British foe and not at fellow Americans.

In the end, the larger issue raised by Wilson seems more interesting to me than Lincoln's call for a political religion of law-abidingness to replace the revolutionary passion of old. Wilson was right to notice the provocative and disconcerting passage in the Lyceum Address where Lincoln notes that the members of "the family of the lion or the tribe of the eagle" thirst and burn for distinction and will attain it "whether at the expense of emancipating slaves, or enslaving freemen" (*TWAL*, 12). Is Lincoln somehow revealing the Caesarian dimensions of his own soul, tempted by distinction at any cost? There are too many stumbling blocks to justify an affirmation of this quite dubious thesis. As Diana Schaub has ably argued, Lincoln gave ample advice to his fellow citizens on how to recognize and stop the Caesars of the world before they enslave and emancipate at will at the service of their own tyrannical self-aggrandizement. He was not their friend in the slightest. Lincoln is rather like the shepherd announced in his great address at Sanitary Fair in Baltimore, Maryland, on April 18, 1864, who drives "the wolf from the sheep's throat" (*TWAL*, 420–22, especially p. 421) even as the enemies of ordered liberty, the aspiring tyrants, denounce him "as the destroyer of liberty."

In his magisterial 1959 book, *The Crisis of the House Divided*, the political philosopher Harry V. Jaffa describes how complex and variegated Lincoln's political psychology really was. This partisan of noble equality and the right of every human being to keep what he has earned "by the sweat of his brow" (*TWAL*, 115) was fully aware of different human and political types: the tyrants who are not bound by justice or the moral law, men who "do not recognize any obligation to what is commonly called morality." These *Übermenschen*, as Jaffa rightly calls them, are in decisive respects "beyond good and evil." Lincoln, the greatest American defender of natural right and of the requirements of mutual accountability and responsibility of free men under both the political and moral law, would later subtly elevate the Declaration of Independence by giving as much emphasis to transcendental duty as he does to the recognition and protection of fundamental rights: "As I would not be a *slave*, so I would not be a *master.* This expresses my idea of democracy" (*TWAL*, 150), he wrote to himself in September 1858. For Jefferson, self-preservation ultimately trumped one's obligation to respect the rights of others, however genuine they were.

Jefferson on Duty and Self-Preservation

The author of the Declaration of Independence knew slavery was wrong and genuinely hoped to see its gradual elimination. But during the slavery controversy of 1819–1820 culminating in the Missouri Compromise of 1820 allowing slavery in some new states and territories and not others, Jefferson frankly acknowledged that Southerners "have the wolf by the ears and we can neither hold him, nor safely let him go. Justice is in one scale and self-preservation in the other." Richard Brookhiser reports in his finely drawn book *Founders' Son: A Life of Abraham Lincoln* that Lincoln disliked Jefferson as a politician who was at once too populist and flexible and hardly a model of civic courage on the slavery question in his waning years. "Lincoln the reasoner seized on the Declaration's self-evident truths" and perhaps gave them greater elevation and transcendental emphasis than its principal author had done. Yet for all his practical equivocations, Jefferson, like Lincoln to his enduring credit, "did not believe that black men, or any men, could justly be held as slaves." That undeniable truth about Jefferson is increasingly denied or obfuscated by the woke among us. Their moral fervor has no time for niceties such as historical truth, so they make up their facts along the way. Rage and truth are hardly compatible.

Jefferson's approach to these matters, antislavery but ultimately too cautious and tepid in addressing the issue, perfectly mirrors the priority given to self-preservation over moral duty (when they happen to come into contradiction) in the opening chapters of John Locke's *Second Treatise on Civil Government*.[4] Writing in 1959, Jaffa saw that Lincoln remained faithful to the antislavery spirit of the Declaration of Independence even as he emphasized one's duties to others as much as rights to be claimed against government. Lincoln, in contrast, Jaffa noted, reminded free men and women "what they must demand of themselves." He did not "refound" America—that surely goes too far—and it would be

---

4 John Locke, *The Second Treatise of Government*, Chapter Two, "Of the State of Nature": "Everyone, as he is bound to preserve himself, and not to quit his station willfully, so by the like reason, when his own preservation comes not in competition, ought he, as much as he can, to preserve the rest of mankind..." The operative phrase is "when his own preservation comes not in competition." Duty is subordinated to self-preservation in the first articulations of modern philosophical liberalism, something Lincoln saw with crystalline clarity. But duty is not ignored or altogether eclipsed.

presumptive and misleading to reduce the Declaration to mere Lockeanism.[5] The peroration of that noble document ends with a soaring appeal with its signatories "pledging their lives, fortunes, and sacred honor" in defense of its claims and in the struggle for American independence rooted in natural rights and indubitable truths. Still, Lincoln aimed higher and in a manner wholly alien to the *Übermenschen* whom he feared would tear down and build up as their power and "thirst for distinction" dictates and requires. Like the philosopher-statesman Cicero, opposing Caesarian despotism in the twilight years of the Roman republic (with no guarantee of success and culminating in ultimate political "martyrdom" in Cicero's case), Lincoln was a "great-souled man" who was committed to defending civilization, decency, and free politics against "the Caesarian destroyer of republics." Lincoln, like Cicero, would never choose dishonorable ambition that wars on natural justice, human decency, and the precious acquisition that is civilization itself. That is to sully the soul by giving in to the lowest passions camouflaged as high political ambition. It is politics of self-assertion lauded by Callicles in Plato's *Gorgias* and not Socratic virtue rooted in temperance, moderation, and self-knowledge.

A Dialectical Affirmation of Equality

On rare but vitally important occasions, democracies need such men of virtue and honorable ambition to preserve and perpetuate

5 A view shared by such diverse figures as the early Harry V. Jaffa, Willmore Kendall, and Gary Wills. In *A New Birth of Freedom: Abraham Lincoln and the Coming of the Civil War* (Lanham, MD: Rowman & Littlefield, 2000), Jaffa, in contrast, emphasizes the essential continuity between Lincoln and the founders. My sense is that the truth lies somewhere between *Crisis of the House Divided*'s marked emphasis on Lincoln's discreet correction and elevation of the founding and *The New Birth of Freedom*'s insistence on the fundamental continuity between Lincoln and the architects of the American political order.

free and civilized human life. Such magnanimous statesmen are the natural opponent of the tyrant, whether "garden variety" or ideological, as Walter Newell calls them in his valuable 2017 book, *Tyrants: Power, Injustice, and Terror*. The magnanimous statesman is a category that Lincoln knew from the inside, so to speak, as did Cicero, Burke, Churchill, and de Gaulle, among others. A democratic egalitarianism that cannot acknowledge the complexity of the soul and the variety of human types is bound to degenerate into either egalitarian complacency or, in due time, an open war on human excellence. As I pointed out in the first chapter of this book, a political science that thoughtlessly and dogmatically reduces rich and varied human motives to an amorphous desire for power has no capacity to distinguish among the magnanimous statesman, the rapacious or ideological tyrant, and the ordinary public servant bereft of the highest ambition but still broadly committed to public service and moral rectitude (which surely has a dignity of its own). As Jaffa remarks, the author of the Gettysburg Address believed wholeheartedly that "all men are created equal," but his affirmation of this simple but profound truth had nothing to do with doctrinaire egalitarianism or a heavy-handed or dogmatic "democratic ideology." His was a more complex and dialectical affirmation of the same truths affirmed in the Declaration of Independence. As the incomparable Gettysburg Address of November 19, 1863, attests, these "self-evident truths" also became a "proposition" and challenge tied to duties and sacrifices at the service of the noble cause of self-government, "government of the people, by the people, for the people" (*TWAL*, 417), a cause that should never be confused with the right of a people to do what they will. That is the principle of mastery, slavery, and despotism, not of a free people governing itself under humanizing limits marked by natural right and divine justice and guided by what Lincoln called in his superb July 6, 1852, eulogy for Senator Henry Clay "human liberty, human right and human nature" (*TWAL*, 43–54 for the speech, 48 for the quotation). Like Clay, Lincoln loved his country "partly because it was his own country, but mostly because it was a free country" (*TWAL*, 48). Like Clay, but with more vigor and determination, he knew that succumbing to the evil sophistry that self-government or "popular sovereignty" included the right to own and sell others "must," in Clay's words from 1827, "blow out the moral lights around us" (quoted in *TWAL*, 53). A policy of moral neutrality toward slavery would "eradicate the light of reason, and the love of liberty" (*TWAL*, 53) among the American people. To go beyond the argument of "necessity" was to "repress all sympathy, and all humane, and benevolent efforts among free men" (*TWAL*, 53). Lincoln's unforced mixture of magnanimity and charity could never accommodate the evil of chattel slavery. And the noble principles and traditions of this country would not allow it. The conservative, Old Whig Abraham Lincoln was as opposed to slavery as any fire-breathing abolitionist. And as Reinhold Niebuhr once wrote, there is no "reason to believe that Abraham Lincoln, the statesman and 'opportunist,'" was "morally inferior" to the allegedly more "prophetic" William Lloyd Garrison (who repeatedly railed against the constitution's compromises with slavery in the pages of *The Liberator*). Prudence at the service of principle may in fact be the quintessence of morality applicable to the political common good. To reduce prudence to Machiavellian manipulation or unprincipled caution is to distort the very meaning of practical reason and the political good.

Lincoln's Intellectual and Political Path

Lincoln, coming from the humblest of backgrounds, was largely self-taught, reading Euclid, Shakespeare, Milton, Blackstone, the

Bible, the American founders, and a wide range of eighteenth- and nineteenth-century writers on law, politics, religion, and political economy. And undoubtedly much more. Politically, he adhered to the Whig Party with its suspicion of vulgar populism and its support for a system of government-supported infrastructure and "internal improvements" such as canals to promote commercial exchange and national economic development. Lincoln believed in the collaboration of capital and labor and was an adherent of the "free soil" movement. The latter supported industriousness as a means of advancement as well as the widespread diffusion of property. All of this was accompanied by an active and heartfelt disdain for slavery.

Lincoln was elected to Congress from the state of Illinois for one term beginning in 1848. As a congressman, he most notably spoke out against the Mexican War, whose justifications seemed spurious to him and whose underlying imperialism provided a cover for the expansion of slavery. His biographers tell us that by the early 1850s, this lawyer for the railroads had largely lost his taste for politics. But the repeal of the Missouri Compromise of 1820 (which still upheld marked limits on the spread of slavery) accomplished by the Kansas-Nebraska Act of 1854 (which opened Kansas and Nebraska to slavery in the guise of "popular sovereignty") stirred his soul to renewed political action.

Lincoln Becomes Fully Lincoln: The Peoria Address

It was in the lengthy speech on the Kansas-Nebraska Act, delivered in Peoria, Illinois, on October 16, 1854, (*TWAL*, 59–92) that Lincoln's convictions crystallized in an eloquent and determined effort to prevent the spread of slavery and to oppose the sophistic and morally corrupting doctrine of "popular sovereignty."

All of Lincoln's mature political convictions can be found in a sustained and articulate form in the Peoria Address. It was the beginning of the journey that would lead to his adherence to the new antislavery Republican Party, to his searing opposition to the Supreme Court's 1857 Dred Scott decision that egregiously denied the humanity of the black man (only white men of European descent were deemed equal in this willful misreading of the Declaration of Independence), and his famous debates with Senator Stephen Douglas (the true architect of the doctrine of "popular sovereignty") that would eventually propel him not to the U.S. Senate, as he initially hoped, but to the presidency of the United States in 1861.

Douglas had repeatedly made the case for the unadulterated will of the stronger, of what Tocqueville famously called "the tyranny of the majority." Lincoln, in contrast, "insisted that the case for popular government depended upon a standard of right and wrong independent of mere opinion and one that was not justified merely by the counting of heads," as Harry Jaffa so well put it. Lincoln saw a moral purpose underlying republican self-government, and as a result, he refused to divorce popular rule from the requirements of natural justice. Therein lies one source of his greatness and why he remains an indispensable educator for democratic peoples.

Lincoln did not mince words: he saw in Senator Douglas's "*declared* indifference" to the spread of slavery a "covert *real* zeal" (*TWAL*, 66) for its spread. This moral indifference made a mockery of the Declaration of Independence, "the sheet anchor of American republicanism" (*TWAL*, 76), as Lincoln called it. For Lincoln, the nub of the matter was the Declaration's claim "that no man is good enough to govern another man, *without that other's consent*" (*TWAL*, 76). And with a powerful dual appeal to reason and the natural moral sense of human beings, Lincoln unequivocally proclaimed the humanity of the black man. The contempt that white Southerners showed toward the dealers in slaves showed as much since nobody objects to commerce in animals or mere economic produce (*TWAL*, 74–75). One can repeal the Missouri Compromise, but one cannot repeal human nature and man's love of justice, Lincoln proclaimed with a certain controlled fervor (*TWAL*, 81). Southerners, he noted, joined Northerners in 1820, "almost unanimously, in declaring the African slave trade piracy, and in annexing to it the punishment of death" (*TWAL*, 74). Lincoln sardonically adds that no one ever "thought of hanging men for catching and selling wild horses, wild buffaloes or wild bears" (*TWAL*, 75). Black men and women were children of God endowed with natural rights. And they had every right to keep what they earned "by the sweat of their brow."

To be sure, Lincoln did not know precisely how to end slavery in the short or intermediate terms. He once placed limited hopes in the resettlement of emancipated blacks in Africa or Central America. But by the time of the Peoria Address, he acknowledged the impracticality and perhaps undesirability of such a scheme. For now, the evil of slavery must be freely acknowledged and its spread to new states and territories prevented before America's "moral lights" truly went out. As he would famously state a few years later in the House Divided Speech, a "government cannot endure, permanently half *slave* and half *free*" (*TWAL*, 126). The human heart knows "that slavery extension is wrong; and out of the abundance of his heart, his mouth will continue to speak" (*TWAL*, 81). Human nature and moral right cannot be *repealed*. This was one of Lincoln's deepest convictions. There is not, and can never be, "MORAL

RIGHT in the enslaving of one man by another" (*TWAL*, 83). This the founders knew, and Lincoln reiterated this searing truth with rare eloquence and force of conviction.

Egregious Misreadings

In *How to Be an Anti-Racist*, the black ideologue and activist Ibram X. Kendi makes one passing reference to Lincoln, quoting, as so many have done out of context, Lincoln's famous letter to Horace Greeley, the editor of the influential *New York Tribune*, dated August 22, 1862. Greeley had chastised Lincoln in the pages of his newspaper for not doing more to immediately put an end to the scourge of slavery. In his response, Lincoln unhesitatingly proclaimed that "If I could save the Union without freeing *any* slave I would do it, and if I could save it by freeing *all* the slaves I would do it; and if I could save it by freeing some and leaving others alone I would also do that" (*TWAL*, 361–62). Kendi predictably sees this as evidence of Lincoln's racism and moral indifference.[6] But Lincoln's critics then and now fail to appreciate that the union that Lincoln was constitutionally pledged to preserve was one that was antislavery to its core. In accord with the dictates of prudence, Lincoln would do what he could in due time to eliminate this inhuman scourge.

The Emancipation Proclamation would follow on the twenty-second day of September 1862, announcing the emancipation of all slaves living in the Confederacy or under "military occupation" (*TWAL*, 395–96) on the first day of January 1863. This bold move was justified by "military necessity" but was surely also

6 Ibram X. Kendi, *How to Be an Antiracist* (New York: One World, 2019), p. 206. Kendi's discussion of Lincoln is so cursory and so dishonest, so bereft of equity, that, in and of itself, it reveals the soul of a censorious ideologue and apparatchik.

informed by deep moral conviction (near the end of the proclamation, Lincoln emphatically calls it an "act of justice," *TWAL*, 396). Soon free blacks would join the Union Army and fight bravely. And as already noted, Lincoln would endorse black suffrage in a speech given just four days before his assassination of April 14, 1865. As Diana Schaub has argued, the "evolution of Lincoln's policy preferences" never "entailed a significant shift of premises." Lincoln always believed that "Blacks, like all people, were capable of self-government." Lincoln had to pay due respect to public opinion, as all statesmen must, but he always led that opinion upward and never catered to its grossest prejudices. This is too often forgotten. Without prudent but principled statesmanship, there could be no movement toward "a new birth of freedom," only moral posturing and impotent rage. As Allen C. Guelzo has argued, because we have forgotten the moral character of prudence rightly understood, we are in danger of severely underestimating Lincoln's moral and political achievement.

From Paine's Skepticism to Biblical Republicanism

The fine Lincoln scholar Joseph R. Fornieri has helpfully referred to "Lincoln's noble vision of democratic government" as "biblical republicanism." There is no reason not to vouchsafe this claim. Lincoln's transcendental affirmation of human liberty and human dignity is unthinkable without biblical charity and a nonsectarian affirmation of Divine Providence. Yet Lincoln belonged to no church and toyed with free-thinking and "rationalist" convictions as a young lawyer and postmaster in Illinois. As Richard Brookhiser has written, the young "Lincoln did more than just talk about religion. When still living in new Salem [Illinois], he wrote a Painite pamphlet explaining that the Bible was not God's word, and Jesus was not His Son. He read it aloud to friends during the slack hours of his postmaster's job, and spoke of getting it printed—until Samuel Hill, an older man who owned one of the village's stores, took the manuscript and burned it." Lincoln may have never had a political career at all if this incendiary document had seen the light of day. Does all this suggest that Lincoln's qualified and dialectical turn toward biblical republicanism was subterfuge and merely an element of a salutary if ultimately Machiavellian civil religion? The answer is no, as I will explain with the help of the scholarship and insights of Allen C. Guelzo and Diana Schaub. But nor did Lincoln, a man of the rarest spiritual depth, become a Christian believer in any simple or orthodox meaning of the word. Therein lies a tale.

Let us begin closer to the beginning. Allen Guelzo has shown, with the help of William Herndon's papers and testimony, that Lincoln the youthful rationalist was also a philosophical fatalist. He was for a time, and perhaps a long time, an adherent of a secular form of predestinarianism that he called "the doctrine of necessity." As Herndon showed, Lincoln believed that human actions were determined by fundamental "motives" over which we have little or no control. Lincoln once told Herndon that "motives moved the man to every voluntary act of life." Lincoln's mistake, if I may dare to call it such, was to sever motives from any exercise of free will or reflective choice. He was for a time fixated by a potent mix of secularized Calvinism and philosophical fatalism.

From the "Doctrine of Necessity" to a (Qualified) Affirmation of Providence

As Lincoln came to vigorously oppose the new pernicious doctrine of "popular sovereignty," which gave individuals and communities the right to choose an egregious, even monstrous, wrong, he more and more appealed to natural law reasoning, as we have seen, to oppose the terrible evil of slavery. These arguments were meant to persuade and thus to change our motives, choices, and judgments. Guelzo has said it best: Lincoln was for much of his adult life "a fatalist who promoted freedom." Confronting as president the massive sacrifices of the American people to preserve union and liberty and in due course to expunge the evil of race-based chattel slavery, Lincoln more and more referred "to 'an all-wise-Providence,' and to 'Divine assistance' without which 'all must fail.'" Theistic Providence, with a touch of predestination, replaced the cold "doctrine of necessity." As Guelzo writes, these invocations of Divine Providence "were too oft repeated"—and too passionate and sincere, I might add—"and the powers [Lincoln] ascribed to providence too absolute to be mere political window-dressing." Providence had its own purposes, but so did the actors on both sides of the bloody and fratricidal Civil War.

Gone, too, was the cheap hostility to revealed religion that marked the at-once jocular and subversive free thinker of the 1830s. In the brief and sublime Gettysburg Address, the greatest political speech since Pericles's Funeral Oration or Henry V's St. Crispin's Day speech in Shakespeare's great history play dedicated to that most significant of kings, Lincoln resolved that after the profound sacrifices of those soldiers who had given "the last full measure of devotion" in defense of the noble proposition that "all men are created equal," their sacrifices must be completed by "a new birth of freedom." But this new birth of freedom is that of a "nation, under God" (*TWAL*, 417). Lincoln's biblical republicanism reached its fruition. As Diana Schaub points out in her unfailingly insightful *His Greatest Speeches: How Lincoln*

Moved the Nation, the God that Lincoln invokes is not exactly Jefferson's "Nature's God." In contrast to the Declaration, Lincoln's "civic religion...brings God closer." The same Lincoln, Schaub points out, issued "three proclamations calling on citizens to observe a Day of National Humiliation, Prayer, and Fasting" even as he made four Thanksgiving Proclamations. As all of this hints (or more than hints in my view) "of a politically active, justice-seeking, providential order, setting certain limits upon human action." This revised understanding of a new dialectic of Providence, natural law, and human purposes will of course reach its sublime culmination in the incomparable Second Inaugural of March 4, 1865. Here Lincoln reaches the heights.

God's Purposes

Let us return to the question of God's purposes in contrast to our own. That theme, at the heart of the Second Inaugural, had already been limned by Lincoln in his brief and somber "Meditation on the Divine Will" (*TWAL*, 362), a piece Lincoln had sketched in early September 1862 as the bloody and destructive Civil War saw no signs of abating. Lincoln begins by noting that "The will of God prevails." The conflict could not continue without God's acquiescence. Each side claims "to act in accordance with the will of God," and one or both may be wrong. He writes, in anticipation of the Second Inaugural, that "[in] the present civil war it is quite possible that God's purpose is something different from the purpose of either party" even as both parties are "human instrumentalities" that affect God's purpose. The statement is filled with conditionals and equivocations: "I am almost ready to say that this is probably true—that God wills this contest, and wills that it shall not end yet." God's likely purpose becomes more abundantly clear in the crucial heart of the Second Inaugural, where Lincoln speculates more forthrightly on God's punitive and redemptive purposes.

Let us turn to this sublime exercise in political theologizing. There is nothing like it in the annals of philosophical-minded statesmanship. In it, poetry and theology meet philosophy and the highest tasks of statesmanship geared to civic reconciliation without forgetting or eschewing the requirements of natural and divine justice. Only a soul touched by the highest manifestations of prudence and grace could achieve what Lincoln achieved on this blessed occasion, one inseparably civic and sacred.

For Lincoln, in the order of time and God's Providence, slavery was the cause of this great and terrible conflict. Each side prayed to the same God and read the same Bible, but "the Almighty has His own purposes" (*TWAL*, 429, for all the remaining quotations from the Second Inaugural). Lincoln was always a scourge of what he called elsewhere "pro-slavery theology" (*TWAL*, 190). In a wringing declaration, he states that "it may seem strange that any men should dare to ask a just God's assistance in wringing their bread from the sweat of other men's faces." But he quickly adds, "but let us judge not that we not be judged." His reference to the sobering words of Christ should not be confused with moral relativism or the moral indifference that today goes by the name of "nonjudgmentalism." Lincoln's God does not hesitate to judge the "offense that is American slavery," so much so that this "terrible war" can be justly perceived as just punishment for "every drop of blood drawn with the lash" for two hundred years or so. In such a description, Lincoln discerns no "departure from those divine attributes" of justice and mercy that "the believers in a Living God always ascribe to Him." Is Lincoln a believer, so understood? Not in any simple sense, perhaps, but certainly in a sublime philosophical sense that is unthinkable without Christianity. We are a long way from Tom Paine's anti-Christian ire.

"With Charity For All"

In the famous peroration of this majestic, heartrending address, Lincoln invokes the highest theological virtue: charity. "With malice toward none; with charity for all; with firmness in the right, as God gives us to see the right, let us strive on to finish the work we are in; to care for him who shall have borne the battle, and for his widow, and his orphan—to do all which may achieve and cherish, a just, and a lasting peace, among ourselves, and with all nations." After the chastisement of a just but mysterious Providence comes the work of binding up the nation's wounds, work to be guided by charity, not vengeance or violence.[7] But Lincoln never asks us to forget the evils of the past. That would be to confuse charity with moral indifference and to ignore the requirements of repentance for grave wrongs done.

Nor did civic reconciliation require any slackening in the national commitment to a "new birth of freedom." Diana Schaub nicely traces "the moral prerequisites for reconstruction" that Lincoln had in mind in the final weeks of his presidency before he was shot in Ford's Theater by the unreconstructed Confederate actor John Wilkes Booth. In a speech delivered five weeks after his inauguration and only four days before his death, Lincoln discussed recent developments in the new free state of Louisiana (*TWAL*, 431–34). He praised plans to offer public education to blacks as well as whites and the first

---

7 For a suggestive account of Lincoln's "politics of love," directed at a largely Christian populace instead of a single-minded emphasis on interests and rights, see Grant Havers, *Lincoln and the Politics of Christian Love* (Columbia, MO: University of Missouri Press, 2009).

moves toward opening "the elective franchise upon the colored man" as well as the white one. Education was the first of these tasks, in Lincoln's view. It was the precondition for meaningful, robust citizenship for black Americans. No more talk of repatriation of black Americans to Africa or a black homeland in some part of Central America, schemes that events had long left behind. Blacks had shed their blood for union and liberty, and they were as American as Lincoln. The man who "loathed and hated slavery" would not rest content with second-class citizenship for American blacks. That was no longer an option, and it never was in accord with justice.

If Lincoln had survived Booth's assassination attempt, he would have promoted Reconstruction with the same mixture of principle and refined and morally serious practical wisdom that guided his struggle against efforts to extend slavery to new states and territories and to save a union "dedicated to the proposition that all men are created equal." The murder of Lincoln had tragic consequences for the fulfillment of the civic tasks he had nobly laid out for the American people. But we should never underestimate the profound accomplishment that was the saving of the union and the emancipation of slaves from unholy bondage. Lincoln, philosopher-statesman, one might suggest, united principle and prudence in a manner worthy of classical wisdom while allowing God's mysterious Providence to guide him in the inner struggles that afflicted his soul. What responsibility this great man bore on his shoulders! As Greg Weiner has argued, Lincoln's greatness, whatever the precise state of his ultimate convictions and the inner recesses of his soul, is unthinkable without drawing on the ennobling resources of both reason and revelation. If other statesman-thinkers we have examined self-consciously brought magnanimity and moderation together in admirable and civically prudent ways, Lincoln brought God's grace and charity to bear on his own soul and the soul of a suffering and divided nation.

Moral Resoluteness without Manicheanism and Self-Righteousness

As Reinhold Niebuhr eloquently argued in *The Irony of American History* (1952), Lincoln managed to combine "moral resoluteness about the immediate issues [the evil of slavery] with a religious awareness of another dimension of meaning and judgment." Lincoln was right to fight the "offence" that was human slavery even as Niebuhr was right to fight Communist totalitarianism in his own time. "Modern communist tyranny is certainly as wrong as the slavery which Lincoln opposed." Lincoln, and Lincoln interpreted by Niebuhr, provide an almost perfect "model of the difficult but not impossible task of remaining loyal and responsible toward the treasures of a free civilization" while never identifying our cause with the Providential cause of God himself. Such is the path between a debilitating and irresponsible moral relativism and a self-righteousness that risks falling into blind and self-destructive Manicheanism.

The Sobering Perspective of Eternity

A final word. The last of the opening epigraphs, the one from the Wisconsin State Fair in September 1859, richly displays Lincoln's ability to judge cherished human things in light of eternity: "And, this, too shall pass away." Every good work, every noble political achievement, is ephemeral. This recognition chastens our pride but reminds us of our task: "and let us hope that it is not *quite* true." By the cultivation of the physical world "beneath and around us" and "the intellectual and moral world among us," Lincoln hopes against hope that "we shall secure an individual, social, and political prosperity and happiness, whose course shall be onward and upward, and which, while the earth endures, shall not pass away."

Lincoln's final words point toward freedom, not fatalism, but a freedom that respects natural limits and what believers (and increasingly Lincoln himself) call the Providence of God. America was blessed to have this sublime, anguished, but charitable soul, a philosopher-statesman of the first rank, as our leader during the gravest crisis to confront our young republic. Due largely to the leadership and poetic and philosophical wisdom of Lincoln, the nation's soul was saved. Can we still be trusted to hold on to it as a sacred trust? Not if we ignore the wisdom of Lincoln and the Founding Fathers who inspired him. The choice is up to us in a union gravely divided once more.

Sources and Suggested Readings

Readers can consult any number of anthologies of Abraham Lincoln's writings. As already noted, I have used *The Writings of Abraham Lincoln*, edited by Steven B. Smith and published by Yale University Press in 2012, because of its thoughtful introduction, its judiciously chosen selections, and its excellent ancillary essays.

I am indebted to Richard Weaver's discerning discussion of Lincoln's "conservatism," rooted in "the argument from definition," in Chapter Four of *The Ethics of Rhetoric* (Brattleboro, VT: Echo Point Books & Media, 1953), especially pp. 87–113. See pp. 112–13 for an account of Lincoln's conservative rather than revolutionary adherence to prudence rooted in "reform according to law."

Joseph R. Fornieri's *Abraham Lincoln: Philosopher Statesman* (Carbondale, IL: Southern Illinois University Press, 2003) helpfully explores Lincoln's "biblical republicanism" (in relation to a greatness of soul open to humility before the Most High). On this, see especially p. 128. Fornieri clearly and intelligently illumines the mixture of principle and high prudence that animated Lincoln's soul and statecraft (see especially p. 59).

I had the great good fortune to read Diana Schaub's *His Greatest Speeches: How Lincoln Moved the Nation* (New York: St. Martin's Press, 2021) in galley form. Her commentary on three of Lincoln's greatest speeches (Lyceum, Gettysburg, and the Second Inaugural) is nearly Lincolnesque in its poetic lucidity and its ability to shine a light on the philosopher-statesman's deepest insights and rhetorical deftness and grace. See p. 45 for an account of Lincoln's warnings against Caesarian despotism, p. 108 for his vision at Gettysburg of "freedom anew," pp. 138–39 for his call for enhanced education and an open franchise to bring black Americans more fully into the civic community, p. 143 for a lucid and insightful discussion of the religious dimensions of the Second Inaugural, and p. 159 for a helpful account of the "moral prerequisites of reconstruction."

Harry V. Jaffa's magisterial *Crisis of the House Divided* (Chicago: The University of Chicago Press, 1959, 1982, 2009) still stands out as the greatest political-philosophical engagement with Lincoln's thought, writing, and soul. The writing is pellucid, the insights deep and sparkling. On the dialectical character of Lincoln's affirmation of the truth that "all men are created equal," see pp. 190, 200, 210–17. On Lincoln's discreet elevation of the Declaration of Independence and his real, if not immediately discernible, differences with Jefferson, see pp. 318–25.

Lewis Lehrman's *Lincoln at Peoria: The Turning Point* (Mechanicsburg, PA: Stackpole Books, 2008) is a reliable, insightful, and exhaustive guide to the subject. In it, political good sense meets reliable political history.

Richard Brookhiser ably relates the story of Lincoln's youthful apostasy from the Christian religion in *Founders' Son: A Life of Abraham Lincoln* (Philadelphia: PA: Basic Books, 2014), especially pp. 53–56. I am also indebted to Brookhiser for his account of Lincoln's debts to and differences with Thomas Jefferson. See pp. 157–65.

Allen C. Guelzo's *Abraham Lincoln: As a Man of Ideas* (Carbondale, IL: Southern Illinois University Press, 2017) has been a constant source of insight, especially on the religious question as relates to necessity and Providence. On the striking paradoxes that inform Lincoln's thought and action, see p. 21. On "the doctrine of necessity," see pp. 30–34. On the link between Lincoln's turn to natural law and his affirmation of a Providence that perhaps rules over the world, see pp. 81–84. On the related connection between prudence and Providence for Lincoln, see pp. 191–92.

I am also indebted to Greg Weiner's *Old Whigs: Burke, Lincoln, and the Politics of Prudence* (New York: Encounter Books, 2019), particularly on the themes of prudence, reason and revolution, the eloquent discussions of Lincoln's defense of natural right, and the grounds of his opposition to slavery in Hadley Arkes's 1986 book *First Things: An Inquiry into the First Principles of Morals and Justice* (Princeton, NJ: Princeton University Press, 1986), especially pp. 24–25, and pp. 36–47.

6

CLEAR-EYED STATESMANSHIP:
WINSTON CHURCHILL,
POLITICAL JUDGMENT, AND
THE 'COURAGE TO SEE'

T he greatness of Winston Churchill continues to shine
through despite the ravages that accompany what Roger
Scruton so strikingly called "the culture of repudiation." To be
sure, there are growing efforts to "cancel" one of the greatest
human beings of this or any other time. One of his best biographers, the English historian Andrew Roberts, has rightly noted
that his conservatism, a conservatism at the service of English
liberty and the broader inheritance of Western civilization, could
be summed up under "the generalized soubriquet, *Imperium et
Libertas,* Empire and Freedom." But "civilizing empire" has a bad
name today and is wrongly and presumptively identified with
plunder and exploitation and a racist contempt for other peoples
and nations. All were alien to Churchill. I will address this theme
in a section to follow centered around Churchill's *The River War*
(1899 for the authoritative edition), an autobiographical work
where adventure meets political and military history and a mea-

sured account of the duties and responsibilities of civilizing empire worthy of the name.

As Roberts points out in his impressive 2018 book, *Churchill: Walking with Destiny*, Churchill was deeply grateful to the millions of Indian subjects of the Crown who volunteered to fight for the cause of civilization during the two world wars of the twentieth century. His opposition to a precipitous granting of independence to what became India and Pakistan was rooted as much in his desire to avoid sectarian strife and unnecessary bloodshed than in imperial blindness to the self-determination of peoples or the dignity of colonial subjects. Churchill was humane and magnanimous if he was anything at all. His fiercest critics are driven by ignorance and ideological *parti pris*, not to mention a lack of gratitude to the statesman, who more than anyone saved Western liberty and made possible Britain's "Finest Hour."

Churchill's Political Judgment

To acknowledge Churchill's greatness does not necessitate hagiography or what Churchill himself called "gush." There is always an essential need and role for "discriminate criticism." Roberts enumerates a long list of issues and decisions in the nine decades of Churchill's life (1874–1965) where his judgment might be legitimately questioned. These include his early opposition to women's suffrage, his decision to continue the Gallipoli operation after March 1915, his employing of the Black and Tan paramilitary forces in Ireland, his support for Edward VIII in the Abdication Crisis of 1936, his mishandling of the Norwegian campaign in the spring of 1940, the misplaced "Gestapo" speech during the 1945 general election campaign that badly backfired (he suggested that Labour-style socialism might eventually require a full-fledged totalitarian apparatus and secret police), and his questionable decision to remain prime minister after a serious stroke in 1953. All these decisions and judgments are debatable, and some were no doubt mistakes, perhaps even serious mistakes.

But much of this is beside the point. Political greatness is not coextensive with infallibility or perfect judgment. On the issues that really mattered, Churchill was right, and not just in 1940 or as a critic of the disastrous appeasement of Hitler's lupine imperialism in the half decade or more before the outbreak of the Second World War. Today, many mediocre historians and critics, professional enemies of the very idea of human greatness, begrudgingly acknowledge that Churchill was right once, in 1940, and never or rarely before or after. These include those with a pronounced leftist orientation as well as the kind of perverse Tories, like the historian John Charmley, who retrospectively have preferred a separate peace with Nazi Germany in order to preserve the British empire and to ward off a coming threat from Soviet Communism. Even the Labour leader Clement Attlee, who presided over the War Cabinet with Churchill during the Second World War and came to acknowledge his qualities and to esteem him as a human being, problematically claimed that "Energy, rather than wisdom, practical judgment or vision, was his supreme qualification." In truth, his undeniable energy would have amounted to very little, or little that was positive and constructive, if it had not been informed by practical wisdom of the first order.

In the magisterial conclusion to *Churchill: Walking with Destiny*, Roberts effectively responds to the naysayers, to those who are intent on minimizing both Churchill's greatness and the practical judgment that informed and vivified that greatness. Roberts rightly points out that "when it came to all three mortal threats posed to Western civilization, by the Prussian militarists in 1914, the Nazis in the 1930s and 1940s and Soviet Communism after the Second World War, Churchill's judgment stood far above that of the people who sneered at his." Paraphrasing Kipling's great poem "If," Roberts notes that many of Churchill's critics were "losing their heads and blaming it on him." Attlee, honorably anti-Nazi to be sure, opposed rearmament and conscription before World War II, long after Churchill had wisely called for both. "Energy, rather than wisdom" indeed.

I would add that Churchill understood the lethal character of Bolshevism long before the majority of his complacent contemporaries. As early as April 11, 1919, in a speech in London, Churchill argued that "Bolshevist tyranny," as he called it, was "the worst, the most destructive, and the most degrading" in human history. He would reiterate that claim many times over the years. Churchill wanted to truly help the fledgling White forces in Russia while his short-sighted colleagues were anxious to withdraw the small Allied forces in Russia who were in a position to prevent the consolidation of Bolshevik tyranny. Even this is held against Churchill by anti-anti-Communist historians, who are legion today. Somehow a meagre, ineffectual, and brief Allied presence on Russian soil during the Russian Civil War is said to be responsible for the long Cold War. This reflects anti-anti-Communist ire rather than a disinterested analysis of the facts. A widely held sophism, but a sophism nonetheless.

Roberts is most effective at challenging the facile and fashionable view that Churchill was a "hedgehog" (to cite the adage of the Greek poet Archilochus, popularized by Isaiah Berlin) who got only one big thing right. In truth, Churchill, no socialist, was in the years before the Great War "the initiator of much social legislation to alleviate the suffering of the grindingly poor of Edwardian Britain." A member of the Liberal Party at the time, his role in creating

a modest British welfare state reflected his Disraeli-like commitment to "one-nation" conservatism, to "Tory Democracy" broadly
understood. Churchill early on saw the need for an effective and
long-term alliance with a France that could no longer adequately
defend herself without external help. As first lord of the Admiralty,
he got the fleet ready for World War I, and he is in many ways
the father of the tank and appreciated, henceforth, the centrality
of tank warfare in modern military operations. He made peace
with the Irish rebel Michael Collins (whom he also befriended)
and helped bring the Irish Free State into existence. During his
second premiership, he renewed the path of Tory Democracy by
building "a million homes and abolishing rationing." These are
considerable achievements, numerous, and in no way simply "one
big thing" at one brief moment in time.

Churchill and the Twin Totalitarian Marauders

Last but not least, Roberts adds, Churchill "was the first significant political figure to spot the twin totalitarian dangers of Communism and Nazism and to point out the best ways of dealing
with both." Roberts thus rightly concludes against Churchill's
critics—not the full-blown "cancelers" but rather the academic
"belittlers"—that "Churchill was a quintessential fox, who knew
and did many things, not a hedgehog." In this judgment, Roberts
is surely right. But one might go on to add that this fox put many
hedgehogs to shame.

In one of his greatest speeches—eloquent, discerning, and
speaking the truth fearlessly and without hesitation amidst a false
sense of "joy and relief"—on the calamity that was the Munich
Pact ("A Total and Unmitigated Defeat," delivered in the House
of Commons on October 5, 1938), Churchill made clear why there

"can never be friendship between the British democracy and the Nazi power, that power which spurns Christian ethics, which cheers its onward course by a barbarous paganism, which vaunts the spirit of aggression and conquest, which derives strength and perverted pleasure from persecution, and uses, as we have seen, with pitiless brutality the threat of murderous force." And then with laconic eloquence he draws the only conclusion that can be drawn from such a situation: "That power cannot ever be the trusted friend of the British democracy." Not appeasement but a "supreme recovery of moral health and martial vigor" is necessary for Britain (and the other democracies) to "take [her] stand for freedom as in the olden time." Here we see and cannot help but admire understanding at the service of eloquence, practical reason at the service of a politics of tough-minded but humane prudence, a defense of freedom at the service of true peace and not pacifism or pusillanimity.[1]

The Courage to See: Saving the West as the West

Churchill saw what was at stake in the totalitarian assault on liberal and Christian civilization like few people before or after. Among twentieth-century statesman, only de Gaulle shared this

---

1 In a brilliant but little-known radio address to the American people in the fall of 1938, Churchill forcefully challenged the illusion that "peace, good will, and confidence" can "be built upon submission to wrong-doing backed by force." He denounced the totalitarian "cult of war," its militarization of human existence, even as he called for "the remaining forces of civilization" to actively resist the new ideological barbarians. Arms must be supported by "words and thoughts" at the service of civilization and political freedom since the totalitarians "make frantic efforts to bar out thoughts and words; they are afraid of the working of the human mind" but are ultimately helpless "to quell the natural promptings of human nature." And quite notably on this occasion, Churchill stated that Communist and Nazi tyranny "are the same thing spelt in different ways." See Winston S. Churchill, "The Defence of Freedom and Peace," in David Bromwich, ed., *Writing Politics: An Anthology* (NYRB Classics, 2020).

admirable lucidity and the determination to resist the inhuman totalitarian temptation on the intellectual, military, political, and spiritual fronts. These two great statesmen fully appreciated that the Second World War was much more than an age-old geopolitical conflict: it was no less than an effort to save and sustain a civilization at once Christian, liberal, and democratic. They still cared for the West as the West, a civilization worth preserving because it alone fully valorized the dignity of human beings who are souls as well as bodies, persons imbued with dignity and not playthings of ideological despotisms that in decisive respects were "beyond good and evil." That noble spiritual and civilizational vision is increasingly moribund in the democracies today.

Churchill always manifested what Aleksandr Solzhenitsyn called "the courage to see." This courage to see is at the heart of Churchill's ability to combine love of peace with truly indomitable courage, resistance to totalitarian aggression with a sincere desire to avoid the "twin marauders" of war and tyranny, as Churchill called them in his Iron Curtain Speech ("The Sinews of Peace," March 5, 1946) delivered at Westminster College in Fulton, Missouri, with President Harry Truman's strong encouragement and support. In that world-famous speech, Churchill celebrated the spiritual and political solidarity of the freedom-loving "English-speaking world," committed as it was "to the principles of freedom and the rights of man which are the joint inheritance of the English-speaking world and which through Magna Carta, the Bill of Rights, the Habeas Corpus, trial by jury, and the English common law find their most famous expression in the American Independence." This is the shared heritage, the spiritual lineage, of the Anglo-American world. It is a particular tradition that reaches out to the universal grounds of liberty and human dignity.

Like one of his greatest inspirations, Edmund Burke, Churchill was a conservative Whig, "an apostle of [ordered] liberty," of constitutionalism built of settled tradition and old wisdom, and a formidable critic of the totalitarian enemies of Western civilization.[2] Churchill and Burke stood equally for modern liberty and ancient wisdom, for Christian ethics and fierce opposition to the totalitarian negation of man, whether Jacobin, Nazi, or Communist.[3] If Burke was the great partisan of a war to the death with Jacobin atheism and tyranny, Churchill advocated "peace through strength," a firm but more cautious and calibrated response to ideological totalitarianism in an age where nuclear weapons could put an end to the human adventure in one fell swoop.

In his "Swan Song" before the House of Commons before retiring as prime minister for a second time ("Never Despair," March 1,

2 In an essay in the October 2006 issue of *The New Criterion*, "Last of the Whigs: Churchill as Historian," Robert Messenger effectively argues that Churchill was "the last of the Whig historians. He believed that the history of England was that of the ceaseless advance of individual liberty. Englishmen fought for their own land, and they fought in foreign lands to preserve and spread it" against Louis XIV, Napoleon, Wilhelm II, and Hitler. True enough. But Messenger's argument must be qualified in important respects. Churchill fully appreciated the fragility of civilized order as well as the threats that standardization and collectivization posed to the integrity of the human soul in a democratic age. If he was a Whig, he was one who had no illusions about the inevitability of "progress." See in particular, his 1925 essay "Mass Effects in Modern Life" in *Thoughts and Adventures: Churchill Reflects on Spies, Cartoons, Flying and the Future*, edited by James W. Muller with Paul H. Courtenay and Alana L. Barton (ISI Books, 2009).

3 Churchill believed that Edmund Burke was the exemplar of true consistency in politics, which he defined as "preserving the same dominating purpose" amidst "changing circumstances." For Churchill, the "the Burke of Liberty" (who stood up to "a domineering Monarch" and sympathized with the American cause) and "the Burke of Authority" (who so eloquently denounced "a brutal mob and a wicked sect" during the French Revolution), was the same man informed by "the same purpose." He was for Churchill the greatest and most noble exemplar of the arts of prudence at the service of civilized liberty. See "Consistently in Politics" in the same edition of *Thought and Adventures*, 42–43. For more on this theme, see Andrew Roberts, "Churchill's Debt to Burke," *The New Criterion* (May 2019).

1955), Churchill defended an independent British nuclear deterrent and hoped that with "patience and courage" the West could survive the age of totalitarianism. Someday, on the distant horizon, "tormented generations" may live to see a new dawn "when fair play, love for one's fellow-men, respect for justice and freedom" are truly the order of the day. That modest but deeply encouraging hope, of course, is by no means preordained according to some logic of historical inevitability (Churchill's political thinking was bereft of such ideological or utopian illusions). In his conclusion to this final parliamentary address as prime minister, Churchill evoked the great Churchillian virtues of hope, determination, and the refusal to surrender or to despair: "Never flinch, never weary, never despair." These were virtues that demanded action and determination on the part of prudent, decent, and freedom-loving men and women. Churchill, a thinking statesman par excellence, combined the Roman virtue of courage with the love of peace and the arts of prudence. And never did he forget that Western liberty was nothing without solicitude for everything represented by "Christian ethics." He is one of history's great avatars and exemplars of "greatness of spirit" informed by decency, prudence, and moderation.

Isaiah Berlin: "Winston Churchill in 1940"

Let us turn now to the most outstanding single piece of writing on the soul, historical imagination, and political achievement of Winston Churchill: Isaiah Berlin's "Winston Churchill in 1940," originally published in *The Atlantic Monthly* in 1949. Berlin spent much of the Second World War as an observer of the American scene for the British government. But he never lost sight of the home front or Churchill's central role in sustaining the cause of

Western liberty. Berlin's magisterial 1949 essay, republished in several anthologies of Berlin's writings, most recently *The Proper Study of Mankind*, gets to the heart of Churchill's moral and political bearing in a manner that academic historians and political scientists cannot begin to convey. With a few notable exceptions, they have lost the capacity to speak about the soul and the rich and diverse motives that inform it.

Where they tend to dogmatically see nothing but broad, inexorable causes at work, Berlin (for all the limits of his "pluralistic" moral philosophy), like Aristotle and Churchill himself, appreciated that history is what "Alcibiades did and suffered." The determinism implicit in the social sciences and what Tocqueville called "fatalistic" or "democratic" history cannot begin to illumine the role that a great soul, for good or for ill, can play in the unfolding of history. As Milton Himmelfarb once declaimed, "No Hitler, no Holocaust." And one can add with equal assurance, "No Churchill, no survival of British liberty or the cause of Western civilization." Berlin, to his enduring credit, was committed wholeheartedly to this golden verity without which there can be no serious thought or noble action.

Berlin begins his essay by recalling a 1928 book on the art of writing English prose by the then well-known poet and critic Herbert Read. Read's book took aim at Churchill's allegedly "high-sounding, redundant, falsely eloquent, declamatory" prose, self-aggrandizing in Read's estimation and false to its very core. Marked by a somber and dissatisfied postwar mood that was critical of everything high-minded, including "noble eloquence" itself, Read deplored Churchill's "grand style." It was at best anachronistic, at worse "hollow pasteboard" that had nothing to say to the dark realities of the time.

Berlin believed that this view, tinged with nihilistic despair, was "profoundly mistaken." Churchill's "heroic" and "highly colored" if "sometimes over-simple and even naïve" rhetoric was the "natural means" for him to express a "genuine" vision of life. Where Read saw an "unconvincing...illusion," Berlin discerned an "inspired, if unconscious, attempt at a revival," one indebted to Gibbon, Dr. Johnson, Peacock, Macaulay, and classics such as Cicero. It was undoubtedly "too bright, too big, too vivid, too unstable for the sensitive and sophisticated epigoni" of the 1920s. Berlin found Read's analysis of Churchill to be unconvincing because it made no effort to understand Churchill from the inside and was blind to the totalitarian threat already visible on the horizon.

Churchill's vivid language, with its "sharply marked characteristics," spoke to the new situation and the courage needed to confront it precisely because it combined formal eloquence with truly "public" language, Ciceronian, dignified, and "remote from the hesitancies and stresses of introspection and private life" that preoccupied intellectuals such as Herbert Read or those young men at Oxford in 1933 who voted to "never again to fight for King and country." Churchill's rhetoric was the medium for bringing together love of liberty with the Roman virtue of courage. When Churchill spoke to the nation on June 4, 1940, ("Wars Are Not Won by Evacuations") after the return of 333,000 allied troops — 26,000 of them French — who had been semi-miraculously rescued from death or captivity at Dunkirk, his Augustan prose conveyed both realism about the situation confronting the British people and the heroic determination to stand up to approaching evil, come what may. It is rhetoric for the ages that stirs souls that can still respond to the clarion calls of honor and liberty. Here is the most memorable and dramatic passage:

> Even though large tracts of Europe and many old and famous
> States have fallen or may fall into the grip of the Gestapo and all

the odious apparatus of Nazi rule, we shall not flag or fail. We shall go on to the end, we shall fight in France, we shall fight on the seas and oceans, we shall fight with growing confidence and growing strength in the air, we shall defend our island, whatever the cost may be, we shall fight on the beaches, we shall fight on the landing grounds, we shall fight in the fields and in the streets, we shall fight in the hills, we shall never surrender.

At the same time, as Britain carried on the struggle with her last breath and the most heroic determination, Churchill had "realistic" hopes that in "God's good time, the new world, with all its power and might, steps forth to the rescue and liberation of the old." No false colors here, no inflated verbiage. Just the noble eloquence and honorable love for political liberty and national independence that was Churchill's hallmark. This inspiring and inspiriting rhetoric allowed a commercial and peace-loving people to stand up to Hitler's monstrous tyranny and ravenous imperialism. In Berlin's words, through noble speech of this kind, Churchill single-handedly "created a heroic mood" and helped give the common cause of Western liberty a "sublimity" that carried the British people through the Battle of Britain. Without vivid, colorful, ennobling, and inspiriting rhetoric of this sort, Churchill would not have won what the historian John Lukacs has rightly called his "duel" with Hitler.

As Berlin points out, Churchill's volumes on the Second World War (six in all) are guided by the same vision, moral imagination, coloration, and ennobling rhetoric. In this moment of supreme crisis, Churchill's world, as Berlin called it, evoked "the primacy of public over private relationships," insisted "upon the supreme value of action," and spoke freely and unapologetically about "the battle between simple good and simple evil, between life and death." No sophisticated relativism or debilitating "moral equivalence." Churchill's public speech dispelled the acids of modernity and restored cardinal virtues such as courage, justice, and fortitude to their rightful place in the souls of human beings. No nihilism here either, only the moral clarity that allows free peoples to fight heroically for freedom and civilization. In this regard Churchill stands with Cicero and Burke as a *defensor civitatis* par excellence, a defender of the human city against the ideological barbarians at the gate.

The Sympathetic Identification with Great People and Nations

In "Winston Churchill in 1940," Isaiah Berlin beautifully captured how Churchill's humane historical and moral imagination allowed him to experience great and ancient nations and peoples from within, so to speak. The Germans were a "great historic race" for Churchill. They were never reducible to the depravity and cruelties of Hitler, "this evil man, this monstrous abortion of hatred and defeat." That is why, among other reasons, he could, generously and magnanimously, call for the "revival of Europe" through a grand partnership between "a spiritually great France and a spiritually great Germany" in his memorable speech on European unity at Zurich on September 19, 1946. Half-American himself (on his mother's side), he studied American history and politics, traveled widely through its states, befriended President Franklin Roosevelt, and became the popular historian of the "English-speaking peoples" (his four volume *History of the English-Speaking Peoples*, essentially completed before the outbreak of the Second World War, was finally published in 1956). In addition, Churchill had what Berlin rightly calls a "glowing vision of France and her culture" and always supported "the necessity of Anglo-French collaboration." If he sometimes saw Russia as half-Asiatic and prone to "oriental despotism," he also appreciated its civilizational and cultural achievements and saw its people as sorry victims of a truly unprecedented totalitarian order.

There is more one can add. In his wartime speeches, Churchill speaks of the subjugated peoples of Europe with a vividness and sympathy that comes from an historical imagination that is vibrant, living, and in no way antiquarian or academic. Near the end of the Finest Hour Speech of June 18, 1940, he speaks of "Czechs, Poles, Norwegians, Dutch, Belgians" who "have joined their causes to our own." He movingly adds with a strikingly biblical resonance: "All shall be restored." Churchill speaks of free peoples, Western peoples, whom he knows well and are vital parts of a civilization, one might say civilization itself, which was then under unprecedented assault. His evocative rhetoric was perfect for this sobering moment and admirably combined realism with hope and a call to action.

This is a rhetoric, wholly "authentic" as Berlin has already established, that truly moves—and elevates—souls. And in the famous passage from the "Iron Curtain" speech of March 5, 1946, where Churchill discusses the Iron Curtain that has descended across half of Europe, he speaks of "the capitals of the ancient states of Central and Eastern Europe"—Warsaw, Berlin, Prague, Vienna, Budapest, Belgrade, Bucharest and Sofia"—with a sympathy and familiarity that is palpable. He *knows* them, he *feels* for them, and he does not want the rest of Europe to experience the dislocations, repressions and persecutions, police states and "totalitarian control," as these great and ancient peoples were already experiencing. No European or American statesman could speak this way today or would know how to. Churchill's is a cosmopolitanism that is essentially conservative, rooted in tradition, historical imagination, and deep sympathy for the myriad national and cultural expressions of civilized Western liberty. His language was much broader and deeper than the reductive contemporary language of "human rights." Churchill was the consummate British patriot but also a "good European" and the most civilized of men.

"A Periclean Reign"

For Berlin, Churchill's "imagination" and "will" were able to lift the British people "to an abnormal height in a [supreme] moment of crisis." He suggestively calls it "a Periclean reign," worthy of the great Athenian statesman Pericles himself, whose admirable statesmanship we know from Thucydides and Plutarch. Churchill's will, moral imagination, and Ciceronian rhetoric, and his broader courage and determination, "transformed cowards into brave men, and so fulfilled the purpose of shining armour." Churchill was the lion who roared and who called to the British people: "Let us therefore brace ourselves to our duties and so bear ourselves that, if the British Empire and its Commonwealth last for a thousand years, men will still say, 'This was their finest hour.'" These words of June 18, 1940, are quintessentially, emblematically, Churchillian and rightly speak to the ages.

But Berlin makes clear that Churchill's noble and evocative rhetoric has nothing to do with "the kind of means by which dictators and demagogues transform peaceful populations into marching armies"; Churchill's noble rhetoric fully operated within "the framework of a free system without destroying or even twisting it." This is perfectly stated. If Churchill was in some respects a romantic, filled with chivalric sentiments and sympathies, he also "was saved... by a sufficiency of that libertarian feeling" that allowed him to fully perceive "what is false, grotesque, contemptible in the great frauds upon the people practiced by totalitarian regimes." He truly loved political liberty and representative government, and he had respect for the dignity of ordinary people, in their simple "cottage homes," as he put it in the Iron Curtain Speech. Of aristocratic lineage himself, he was no crude snob, as his best biographers well attest. He was an anti-totalitarian through and through. He "mobilized the English language," as the American journalist Edward R. Murrow famously put it, in no small part to expose monstrous pretensions of the totalitarians. Churchill admirably combined astute analysis with eloquence and a call to arms as in these famous sentences, at once instructive and ennobling, from the peroration of the Finest Hour Speech:

> Hitler knows that he will have to break us in this island or lose the war. If we can stand up to him, all Europe may be free, and the life of the world may move forward into broad, sunlit uplands. But if we fail, then the whole world, including the United States, including all that we have known and cared for, will sink into the abyss of a new Dark Age made more sinister, and perhaps more protracted, by the lights of perverted science.

Churchill's remarkable combination of Periclean greatness with a Ciceronian rhetoric educated in liberty and civic virtue was committed to a libertarian civilization informed by mercy and chivalry, one that inherited an elementary decency from the Christian centuries. This rare mixture of virtues and perspectives helps explain Churchill's abiding greatness. Writing in 1949, Isaiah Berlin, a most literate and discerning eyewitness to Churchill in 1940, rightly concluded that Churchill was "an orator of prodigious powers, the saviour of his country, a mythical hero who belongs to legend as much as reality, the largest human being of our time."

This is not the aforementioned "gush" or hyperbole but rather empirical description of a very high order, utilizing the full poetic resources of the English language to capture the deepest recesses of the statesman's soul.

Those words will continue to ring true. Isaiah Berlin's witness to Churchillian greatness, shorn of cynicism and the modern intellectual's tendency to repudiate and tear down the noble and exemplary, is a gift for this and coming generations. It captures the phenomenon of "greatness of spirit" with eloquence, seriousness, and gratitude, and with a rare literary and moral grace and acumen appropriate to the subject.

"A Man of Destiny"

Like Charles de Gaulle, Churchill saw himself from his teenage years as a "man of destiny." Andrew Roberts reports that Churchill told a teenage friend that he was destined for great things and would one day save London from occupation and destruction, even as de Gaulle wrote an essay in 1905 foreseeing that in the year 1930 (he was a mere ten years off!), "General de Gaulle" would save France and Europe from tyranny and aggression.[4]

---

4 Churchill's father, the statesman Randolph Churchill, who died prematurely in 1895, did not share this confidence. He thought his son Winston mediocre and worried about his future. In a "private article," published posthumously in 1966 as "The Dream," Churchill reports a 'visitation' he had from his father as Winston repaired a portrait of him at Chartwell, Churchill's home, in November 1947. In the course of an engaging "conversation" about everything that had happened since 1895—the two world wars, the survival of the British monarchy, women's suffrage, the lethal threats from and monstrous tyranny of Nazism and Communism, the rise of the United States, his own career as a writer and journalist—Churchill only fails to mention his own central role in these dramatic events. In the course of the dialogue, Churchill has his father remark: "As I listened to you unfolding these fearful facts, you seemed to know a great deal about them. I never expected that you would develop so far and so fully. Of course, you are too old now to think about such things, but when I hear you

Readers of *The Gathering Storm*, the first and most gripping of the six volumes of *The Second World War*, well remember the supreme self-confidence that Churchill displayed upon becoming prime minister of Great Britain on May 10, 1940, since he at last "had the authority to give directions over the whole scene." He felt, he told his readers, that he was a man "walking with Destiny, and that all my past life had been but a preparation for this hour and this trial." His predictions "were now so terribly vindicated, that no one could gainsay me." He added that he "could not be reproached either for making the war or with want of preparation for it." Churchill was sure "he would not fail." This is the self-confidence that accompanies genuine magnanimity, or greatness of spirit. Churchill adds that he "slept soundly throughout the war, even during the blitz, "and had no need for cheering dreams." He memorably concludes, "Facts are better than dreams."[5] Noble and humane "greatness of spirit," informed by practical wisdom and true moderation, is indeed a "moral fact" of a very high order. There can be no authentic political science, no genuine understanding of human beings and society,

---

talk I really wonder you didn't go into politics. You might have done a lot to help. You might even have made a name for yourself." After giving Winston "a benignant smile," the "illusion...passed."

"The Dream" is charming and instructive, even endearing. It quietly reveals Churchill's humane and magnanimous self-confidence. See Sir Winston Churchill, *The Dream*, Introduction by Richard Langworth, Afterword by his grandson Winston S. Churchill (Levenger Press, 2005).

5 As the great British journalist and man of letters Malcolm Muggeridge wrote in his diary for June 11–12, 1949: Churchill's "pleasantest feature is that he never attempts for a moment to disguise his great love of exercising authority. No tendency whatsoever to dramatize himself as a man longing for retirement dragged unwillingly into the centre of the stage. He loves, and he says he loves, the limelight. This is most refreshing. He obviously loved every moment of the war, and perhaps was happiest in the days of the blitz." See *Like It Was: The Diaries of Malcolm Muggeridge*, selected and edited by John Bright-Holmes (William Morrow and Company, 1982), 341.

without a willingness to give the proper conjugation of greatness, courage, and moderation its due.

――――――

The River War: To Conquer with Chivalry and Mercy

To sum up: Winston Spencer Churchill was one of the greatest
men of the past century and of modern times more broadly. A
world-class statesman, he embodied the cardinal virtues of courage and prudence. This was once the nearly universal consensus
of free and informed opinion, often accompanied by genuine
admiration and gratitude. To be sure, there have always been out-
liers: inveterate British socialists, eccentric Tory historians who
still defend the wisdom of appeasement, isolationists and pacifists
of various stripes, and anti-anti-Communists who cannot forgive
Churchill for his lucidity about totalitarianism in all its forms.
Today, however, Churchill's cultured despisers have become main-
stream. They take aim at Churchill's alleged racism, his support for
the irredeemably evil West, and his defense of what the political
scientist Kirk Emmert called "civilizing empire."

For example, presenters at a recent conference at Churchill College, Cambridge competed with each other to suggest that Churchill was as bad as if not worse than Adolf Hitler himself. His
grandson Nicholas Soames has asked for Churchill College to be
renamed since this egregious assault on its namesake belies the
considerable benefits it accrues from bearing the name.

James W. Muller's splendid new two-volume edition of Churchill's *The River War*, the first unabridged print edition since 1899,
reveals that there is little or nothing to support such standard-is-

sue charges of racism and hate.[6] Years in the making, delayed innumerable times, this publication of the unabridged *River War* is an event of real significance. The edition's remarkably comprehensive annotations, its helpful maps and beautiful artwork, and above all Muller's lucid and authoritative "Editor's Introduction" (the size of a modest book but without a wasted word) allow us to understand Churchill as he understood himself.

After participating as a soldier-journalist in the Anglo-Egyptian expedition to the Sudan, including joining in the British Army's last full cavalry charge, Churchill spent a year researching and writing his weighty masterwork. Subtitled *An Historical Account of the Reconquest of the Soudan*, it was a labor of love on the part of a brilliant and ambitious young man. Read with a modicum of care (or read at all), *The River War* displays Churchill's remarkable capacity to judge Britain's imperial adventures from the heights with neither uncritical praise nor facile condemnation. Early on in Volume 1, Churchill endorses "the reclamation from barbarism of fertile regions and large populations." But this "wonderful cloudland of aspiration," as he calls it, cannot escape "the ugly scaffolding of attempt and achievement" marked by "the greedy trader, the ambitious soldier, and the lying speculator" (*TRW*, I, 18–19). This British patriot never obscured the moral complexity of human affairs. There was something of Xenophon about Churchill: a soldier, writer, and thinker who combined the spirit of adventure with impressive philosophical equanimity.

Muller, a professor of political science at the University of Alaska, Anchorage presents the full text of the first edition, published when Churchill was only twenty-five and largely forgotten

---

6 All quotations or citations from this authoritative, unabridged edition of *The River War*, published by St. Augustine's Press in 2021 are cited parenthetically in the body of the text as *TRW* followed by the volume number (I or II) and the appropriate page number or numbers.

until Muller stumbled across it in 1989. Churchill's powers of thought and composition are on full display in this version. The prose is, in Muller's words, somewhat "breathless and wordy" (*TRW*, I, clviii) though less rollicking and grandiloquent than some of Churchill's later writing. None of this is a criticism: *The River War* is recognizably Churchillian and a joy to read. Muller uses red font to indicate what was omitted in the second, much more concise edition. Muller points out that this later version is more "stately and reserved" (*TRW*, I, clviii). But it eliminates some observations of great interest and many of Churchill's sharper criticisms of leading figures on the British side—including Lord Herbert Kitchener, the "Sirdar" or commander-in-chief of the Anglo-Egyptian Army, who led the reconquest of the Sudan between 1896 and 1899. Churchill thought Kitchener "a great and splendid figure" but one who "cared little for others" and "treated all men like machines." He was "stern and unpitying," expressing little interest in wounded Egyptian or British servicemen (*TRW*, II, 353–54). Churchill's judgment of Kitchener is far from flattering but eminently fair—if rather bold for a young soldier.

The Sudanese Dervishes, as the British called them (they called themselves the Ansar, "helpers" or "companions" of the prophet Muhammad), rebelled against Egyptian and British rule starting in 1881. Muller notes that this "was an early instance of political Islam, a sort of Muslim revivalism, in collision with Western modernity" (*TRW*, I, xl). This gives Churchill's account a remarkable pertinence to the present day. Churchill admits the Egyptians treated the Sudanese very poorly, even as the Sudanese Arabs enslaved and oppressed the blacks among them. Leading the rebellion against Egyptian rule was Mohammed Ahmed. Ahmed declared himself the "Mahdi," the promised redeemer of the Islamic world. His messianic Islam was often cruel and tyrannical. He died shortly after the triumph of his cause in 1885. The Dervish empire that succeeded him was, in Churchill's estimation, the "worst" that "history records." Its only virtue was courage, real and palpable but severed from both liberty and other "compensating virtues." Still, Churchill gives the Mahdi credit for "rous[ing] patriotism and religion" in the souls of the tribesmen he commanded. Perhaps he was "a commonplace religious impostor." But perhaps in the long run his vision would have given rise to a more tolerable political order. Despite everything, Churchill does not hesitate to call Ahmed "the foremost among the heroes of the race" (for these citations see *TRW*, I, 54–55).

Churchill also recognizes the considerable merits of General Charles George Gordon (also known as Gordon Pasha), whom the British sent to oversee Egypt's withdrawal from the Sudan. In 1885, Gordon lost his life in the city of Khartoum. Mahdist forces overwhelmed his palace as Prime Minister William Gladstone's government dithered about coming to his rescue. Gordon was an accomplished general as well as a man of deep principle and Christian faith. He had warred on slavery in the Sudanese territories out of a deep respect for the dignity of all persons. But his moral rectitude and prideful self-assurance led to imprudence and an excessive confidence in his own judgment. Churchill's final assessment of Gordon is respectful with an undercurrent of doubt and criticism. He was, in Churchill's estimation, "a man of stainless honour and enduring courage," and "the severity of his religion did not impair the amiability of his character." His opinions were not always sound, but "the justice of his actions" (*TRW*, I, 90–104) was generally beyond dispute.

In 1895, a new Conservative and Unionist government under Lord Salisbury officially committed itself to the reconquest of the Sudan. Churchill did not question that goal, but he interrogated some of the motives that inspired it. Certain men of influence and capacity at home and throughout the empire were dominated by a "military spirit" committed to restoring the honor of an empire sullied by the events of 1885. Others, Christians who saw General Gordon as a religious martyr, "sought to avenge his death"; they were given to fanaticism and itched for a "holy war" (*TRW*, I, 164). Still others hoped to bring civilization and sound administration to the suffering people of the Sudan. All these impulses coalesced in what Muller calls a "carefully planned, methodically lengthy, and often tedious operation, well-suited to the temper and talents of the Sirdar who commanded it" (*TRW*, I, lxxi). Churchill supported this effort, but he warned against hubris and also against the potentially cruel and fanatical urge to avenge Gordon's death.

Churchill artfully renders every step of the Sudan's reconquest. As his late daughter Lady Soames points out in her charming foreword, *The River War* beautifully illustrates his "lifelong admiration for courage in friend and foe" as well as the "ordeals and perils on the battlefield" (Soames, *TRW*, I, xiv). These included what Churchill calls "some of the most peculiar and disgusting maladies known to science," such as the unspeakably painful "ferntit" or guinea worm that afflicted many troops on both sides (*TRW*, I, 420). But Churchill also describes the bonhomie among the troops, telling stories or sharing a bottle of champagne. British soldiers during the River War experienced nothing like the inhumanity of the trenches during the interminable years of the Great War.

Soames and Muller both point out Churchill's delight in describing the Desert Railway that Kitchener built, which, despite a setback or two, kept the Anglo-Egyptian armies well supplied as they moved through fierce and forbidding desert (Soames, *TRW*, xii). Some thought the effort to build such a railway in the desert was sheer lunacy. But Churchill appreciated the ambition and the overwhelming eventual success of Kitchener's initiative. Churchill saw romance in the works of modern technology even if he never identified them simplistically with moral progress. He counterbalances his scientific enthusiasm with wonder at the natural world: the Nile River plays a pivotal role in the unfolding of the drama. As Churchill eloquently writes near the beginning of Volume 1, "It is the life of the lands through which it flows. It is the cause of the war. It is the means by which we fight; the end at which we aim." Empires and regimes come and go, but the "great river," which "has befriended all races and every age," endures and reminds us of the limits of our plans and adventures (*TRW*, I, 7–8). Churchill displays piety before nature and a regard for eternity, not just the here and now.

There is a long passage in Volume 2 (excised from the second edition) that comments forcefully and frankly on the "fanatical frenzy" and "fearful fatalistic apathy" inherent in political Islam. Churchill speaks of a "degraded sensualism" that has affected almost every Islamic land. He laments that women are regarded as "absolute property" of men under Muslim law even as he acknowledges that "individual Moslems may show splendid qualities" and have served the queen as "brave and loyal soldiers" (*TRW*, II, 227). This is the sort of passage that has earned Churchill condemnation in our censorious age. Of course, no small number of Enlightenment thinkers said harsher things about Christianity (e.g., Voltaire: "crush the infamous thing"). But the real issue is whether Churchill was right, not whether he offended Muslim sensibilities.

Cancel culture's tyrants go searching for provocative passages as an excuse for un-personing great thinkers and leaders; this has been Churchill's fate. But there is no justification for such obscene displays of ingratitude and efforts at cultural suicide. They are unjust and rest on a terrible simplification. Woke critics fail to read Churchill's thought as a whole or to consider the more provocative passages with the seriousness they deserve. As Muller points out, Churchill defends the rights of women and also makes "a bold and unequivocal criticism of his commander in chief for the way the Sirdar treated the tomb and the remains of the Mahdi" as well as for allowing Dervishes to be killed by his victorious troops (*TRW*, I, cxx). Kitchener did not order this, of course, but he didn't do nearly enough to prevent it. In Chapter 21 of Volume 2 ("After the Victory"), Churchill expresses horror that Kitchener allowed the Mahdi's tomb to be shelled and despoiled. The Mahdi's head was separated from his body and tossed around like an "interesting trophy" until Evelyn Baring, Lord Cromer, ordered its return to Khartoum. "Such was the chivalry of the conquerors!" proclaims an exasperated Churchill (*TRW*, II, 193–94).

As Muller justly remarks, "these are not the views and actions of a man who has casual contempt for other races" (*TRW*, I, cxxx-cxxxi). Churchill always regarded the enemy as human beings capable of displaying courage and heroism. A "racist" or unthinking imperialist he surely was not. Like Edmund Burke before him, who deplored Warren Hastings's crimes and excesses as governor of India, Churchill always called for restraint and respect in governing the peoples of the empire. Muller thoughtfully notes that Churchill's attitude reminds one of "Macaulay's warning in his 1841 essay on Warren Hastings, which Churchill had read in India, about 'the strength of civilization without its mercy.'" Here one breathes the humanizing spirit of Cicero, Burke, Macaulay, and Churchill himself: the spirit of magnanimity tied to moderation, restraint, and mercy.

The River War is the work of a great statesman and thinker, a writer of consequence about issues (empire, Islam, and the clash of civilizations) that remain very much our own. Already in the first edition, Churchill demonstrated the greatness that lay before him.

Churchill, Destiny, and Providence

Britain has had its share of politicians and statesmen who have been "vocal about their faith," from the earnest, evangelical William Wilberforce (with his noble, indefatigable, and ultimately successful fight against slavery and the slave trade) and the tough-minded Methodist Margaret Thatcher to the rather progressive Catholic convert Tony Blair. As the intellectual historian Gary Scott Smith shows in his welcome new book *Duty and Destiny: The Life and Faith of Winston Churchill*, Churchill is not among them.[7]

The great statesman's religious convictions remained to the end somewhat enigmatic, even elusive. Yet Smith's succinct but exhaustive survey of the matter demonstrates that two positions can be safely ruled out: Churchill was neither an atheist (except for a brief if intense period of unbelief in his youth) nor an orthodox Christian who affirmed the Trinitarian God and the divinity of Jesus Christ (*DD*, 181). The distinguished historian and Churchill scholar John Lukacs, himself a Catholic of serious conviction, sees Churchill as above all a pagan in the noblest classical sense

---

7 See Gary Scott Smith, *Duty and Destiny: The Life and Faith of Winston Churchill* (Grand Rapids: MI: William B. Eerdmans, 2021.) All quotations are cited parenthetically in the body of the text as *DD* followed by the appropriate page number.

even if his moral convictions were shaped in important respects by Christianity. There is some truth to this. But Churchill's magnanimity, a quintessentially and initially pagan virtue, was always accompanied by a sense of mercy, chivalry, duty, fair play, and concern for the "humble masses" in their "cottage homes" that took the hardest edges off of classical pride.

As Smith, Paul Johnson, and Paul Addison all emphasize, Churchill had genuine solicitude for the fate of the poor, the "small man," "the underdog," a solicitude that led him to promote salutary welfare measures as a minister in a liberal government during the Edwardian period at the beginning of the twentieth century. He strongly opposed socialism but supported a modest but vigorous welfare state to "help the poor and the working class" (*DD*, 60). Churchill was magnanimous and chivalric in a way that owes much to the precious inheritance that is Christian ethics: his greatness of soul was marked by generosity, kindness, and a concern for the common good. Like the pagan Cicero and the Christian Edmund Burke, his soul impressively melded together magnanimity and moderation, heroic greatness with solicitude for political liberty and the survival and sustenance of civilized order. His capacious soul had ample room for the full range of the classical and the Christian virtues and for a high-minded conception of democracy that did not reject the necessary "continuity" of civilization. He did not reject democracy; he aimed to ennoble it within the limits of the possible. Like Burke, he was a man of high and principled prudence.

Abandoning Atheism

Rather like Abraham Lincoln before him, Churchill often used "Fate," "Destiny," "Providence," and "God" interchangeably in his speeches, writings, and correspondence. Even as a fevered young atheist in the Sudan in 1898 and in South Africa a year or two later fighting in the Boer War (he had abandoned his conventional, tepid Anglicanism after reading the likes of Edward Gibbon, William Lecky, and William Winwood Reade—all pronounced rationalists committed to exposing Christianity as a pernicious superstition), Churchill saw a "Higher Power" at work protecting him from injury and death (*DD*, 9). It was Providence that guided him in his improbable, heroic escape from Boer captivity. For a time, it can be said, Churchill believed in some benevolent "Destiny" or "Providence" looking after him, even if he did not necessarily identify that "Fate" with the God of the Bible or even the God of the philosophers. But even in his period of militant rationalism, which was comparatively short-lived, he did not want to "écrasez l'infâme" ("crush the infamy"—revealed religion—à la Voltaire). Commenting at this time on Gibbon's desire to prove Christianity both false and pernicious, Churchill acknowledged "Toute vérité n'est pas bonne à dire"—"Not all truths should be spoken" (*DD*, 43–44). Churchill was never prone to fiery extremism or political irresponsibility.

Soon enough, Churchill discovered the limits of histrionic rationalism. He came to see that Christianity and all the great religions speak above all to the whole soul, to the whole human person. Smith quotes a Pascal-inspired remark of Churchill from *My Early Life* (1930): "It seemed...very foolish to discard the reasons of the heart for those of the head." Such a balanced reassessment, Smith shows, prompted Churchill to repudiate his juvenile atheism: "The Supreme Creator, who gave us our minds as well as our souls," he concluded, would not "be offended if they did not always run smoothly together in double harness. After all He must have foreseen this from the beginning and of course

He would understand it all" (*DD*, 44–45). Writing to his wife, Clementine, in 1928, long after he had outgrown his youthful skepticism, Churchill lamented that his son Randolph was for the moment attached to a rabid and obnoxious agnosticism and thus risked making a "nuisance" of himself (*DD*, 181).

In his splendid essay on Moses in *Thoughts and Adventures* (1932), Churchill showed his annoyance at "purely rationalistic and scientific explanations" (quoted in *DD*, 86) of the Bible that miss its deeper spiritual truths. Churchill did not doubt the greatest miracle of all: "This wandering tribe, in many respects indistinguishable from numberless nomadic communities, grasped and proclaimed the idea of which all the genius of Greece and all the power of Rome were incapable. There was to be only one God, a universal God, a God of nations, a just God, a God who would punish in another world a wicked man dying rich and prosperous, a God from whose service the good of the humble and weak and the poor was inseparable" (*DD*, 86). This is a truth and insight that Churchill seemed to affirm and for which he had the greatest respect and appreciation. He had come a long way, indeed, from facile rationalism and atheism.

Defender of Christian Civilization

It is in his immense struggle with what he called "the non-god religions" of Communism and Nazism that Churchill's defense of Christian ethics and Christian civilization became most pronounced. Both of these totalist ideologies "substituted the devil for God and hatred for love," as Churchill strikingly put it in a speech in 1936 (*DD*, 100–01). They "spurned Christian ethics" and viciously persecuted Christians (especially Bolshevism) and Jews (especially Nazism). In his great speech on October 5, 1938, assailing the Munich Pact, Churchill denounced Nazism for its "barbarous paganism" (we are a long way from the noble paganism of the classics) that "exalted 'the spirit of aggression and conquest' and that derived 'strength and perverted pleasure from persecution'" (*DD*, 83).

In his greatest wartime address, the Finest Hour Speech of June 18, 1940, Churchill linked success in the Battle of Britain (this as France was falling to Nazi captivity) to "the survival of Christian civilization" (*DD*, 93–94). Not democracy or liberalism per se but the Christian civilization that saw in each precious soul "the image of God" and that called on us to treat other human persons with a modicum of respect, charity, and decency. This was the civilization that called forth noble displays of mercy, forgiveness, and reconciliation. Not even classical paganism at its best—say, Aristotle, Cicero, and the Stoics—could claim that. In Nazism and Communism, Churchill saw a satanic repudiation of human liberty and human dignity, a repudiation at one and the same time of Christian ethics and modern liberty. The two, in Churchill's estimation, stood or fell together.

Scott cites the notable intellectual historian of English religion and politics Maurice Cowling as saying that the youthful Churchill was "uncertain whether transcendental right existed" (*DD*, 48). Not so the mature Churchill. Even in *The River War* (1899), according to Smith, Churchill had "affirmed his belief in transcendent truth and absolute moral standards that were not relative to particular times and places" (*DD*, 157). Human beings in all times and climes desired, in Churchill's words, "to associate their actions with at least the appearance of moral right. However distorted may be their conception of virtue, however feeble their efforts to attain even to their own ideals, it is a pleasing feature and hopeful augury that they should wish to be justified. . . . It is an involuntary tribute, the humble tribute of imperfect beings, to the eternal Temples of Truth and Beauty" (*DD*, 157). Is there a more eloquent account of the stirrings of moral right and natural conscience in the human heart or soul or of the experiences that give rise to an affirmation of natural justice and transcendental truth and beauty?

Let us return to Churchill's moral bearing, a bearing that is at once classical and Christian in the substantial place it finds for honor, courage, duty, and goodwill. The same man who stirred men's souls with his noble call to "Never Surrender!" to a barbarous and totalitarian Nazi Germany once said that if Jesus came back to earth again, he suspected that he might first go "to the untouchables of India" in order "to give them the tidings that not only are all men equal in the sight of God, but that for the weak and poor and downtrodden a double blessing is reserved" (*DD*, 153). Churchill was a magnanimous man, but not the haughty and self-sufficient "magnanimous man" of Aristotle whom I discussed in Chapter Two, whose virtue and pride hardly coexist with generous fellow feeling.

Gary Scott Smith should be commended for making available all the crucial evidence regarding Churchill, religion, and the life of the soul. I think he is right that the great Churchill was, in the end, neither an atheist nor an orthodox Christian. He is right that the divinity of Christ plays no major role in Churchill's thought or his sundry reflections on religion. Perhaps Smith is even right that in some technical sense Churchill was a Unitarian, although hardly of the morally undemanding and self-parodically politically progressive kind that we see around us. But in the end, Churchill's soul is perhaps more interesting, more revealing, than his formal and somewhat elusive religious convictions. That soul and its admirable mix of magnanimity and moderation, to repeat, is unthinkable without the Christianity that Churchill could never bring himself to reject.

Sources and Suggested Readings

Students of Churchill have no shortage of thoughtful, thorough, and astute biographies to choose from. The biographies by Martin Gilbert (in long and short form) and the more compact one by Geoffrey Best are particularly recommended. The most vivid and inviting of the Churchill biographies is the most recent one: Andrew Roberts's *Churchill: Walking with Destiny* (Viking/Penguin, 2018, and 2019 for the paperback edition). I have drawn extensively on the magisterial Conclusion to that book, "Walking With Destiny," pp. 965–82, particularly pp. 965–67, pp. 970–71, pp. 972–73, p. 975, pp. 976–77, and pp. 978–80.

I have quoted extensively from Isaiah Berlin, "Winston Churchill in 1940," in Berlin, Henry Hardy, editor, *The Proper Study of Mankind: An Anthology of Essays* (Farrar, Straus, and Giroux, 2000), pp. 605–27. In my view, this is the most moving and insightful of Berlin's essays, matched only by his entrancing "Conversations with Anna Akhmatova and Boris Pasternak" in the same volume.

All of Churchill's speeches quoted or cited—the 1911 speech on the Bolshevik menace, the great address from 1938 on the "Total and Unmitigated Defeat" that was Munich, the "Blood, Toil, Tears and Sweat" speech of May 13, 1940, the Dunkirk speech of June 4, 1940, the Finest Hour Speech of June 18, 1940, the Iron Curtain and Zurich addresses from the spring and fall of 1946, respectively, and the "Swan Song" to Parliament in 1955 ("Never Despair")—are drawn from Winston Churchill, *Blood, Toil, Tears and Sweat: The Great Speeches* (Penguin, 2007 for the paperback edition). This judiciously selected volume of speeches, edited by the historian David Cannadine, is truly indispensable for the understanding of Churchill and the twentieth century more broadly.

Every student of Churchill's life and statecraft should be familiar with *The Second World War*, especially the first volume, *The Gathering Storm* (Houghton Mifflin, 1948), especially Chapter 1, "The Follies of the Victors: 1919–1929," pp. 3–18 and Chapter 17, "The Tragedy of Munich," pp. 298–321. The golden final paragraph to this volume—"Facts are better than dreams"—can be found on p. 667.

For a vivid and revealing display of Churchill's literary artistry at work, see "The Dream" and my discussion of it in footnote 39 of this chapter. I am indebted to Paul K. Akron's discussion of "The Dream" in his book *Winston Churchill's Imagination* (Bucknell University Press, 2006) and to Andrew Roberts's discussion of it in *Churchill: Walking with Destiny*, pp. 904–06.

=== 7 ===

'THE BORN PROTECTOR': DE GAULLE AS STATESMAN AND THINKER

Charles de Gaulle was perhaps the most impressive states-man-thinker of the twentieth century. His only possible rival in this regard is Winston Churchill, though Churchill presided over a longstanding, stable, and free political order in the United Kingdom, something on which de Gaulle could not depend in the French case. De Gaulle has been the subject of fine biographies in the past, among them a somewhat mythologizing three-volume work by Jean Lacouture, a well-researched but less than sympathetic account by Eric Roussel (who clearly prefers the supranationalist Jean Monnet to de Gaulle's passionate partisanship for the nation), and a more popular and readable account in English by Jonathan Fenby. Added to these now is this superb and equitable portrait by the British historian of twentieth-century France Julian Jackson.[1] In the following pages, we will

---

1 *De Gaulle*, by Julian Jackson (Belknap Press of Harvard University, 2018). The book comes in at 928 pages. It will be cited parenthetically throughout as *JJ* followed by the relevant page numbers.

take Jackson as our initial guide to the thought and action of the great French statesman.

Jackson respects, even admires, de Gaulle but never succumbs to hagiography. He allows de Gaulle's greatness to speak for itself and treats the general's writings and military, political, and philosophical reflections with the seriousness they deserve. His judgments on de Gaulle's thought and statecraft are almost always illuminating and always measured. For all these reasons, Jackson's is likely to remain the authoritative biography of de Gaulle.

Jackson recognizes that, for de Gaulle, "word" and "deed" were inseparable. De Gaulle's prewar writings, especially *The Enemy's House Divided* (1924) and *The Edge of the Sword* (1932), are important sources for understanding his thought and character. That he came from a dignified, Catholic, bourgeois background—one that was, to cite Jackson, "austere, traditionalist, suspicious of ostentation" (*JJ*, 10)—is also relevant. This milieu was nostalgic for monarchy without hating the Republic, wary of revolutionary excess, and open to a middle path between a liberalism that often ignored the needs of the soul and the dehumanizing tyranny that inevitably accompanied socialism. Yet if De Gaulle was *influenced* by these origins, he was not reducible to them.

As a young man and officer, de Gaulle read widely, forming what would become his mature view of France, the world, politics, and the soul. From the French Catholic poet and philosopher Charles Péguy ("an author who mattered immensely to de Gaulle," *JJ*, 20), he learned a generous patriotism that tried to bring together the best of France before and after 1789. Like Péguy, de Gaulle loathed pacifism and loved France. He drew upon Péguy's admiration for Joan of Arc, the saint and warrior who loved God and France with almost equal fervor. For de Gaulle, again like Péguy, France had a "mystical vocation" to bring liberty, civilization, and enlightenment to humanity: in his words, it had "an eminent and exceptional destiny" (cited in *JJ*, 21). This Catholic patriot never succumbed to anti-Semitism any more than he confused the martial virtues, noble within their own sphere, with hatred of other peoples and nations. Totalitarianism of the left and right was never a temptation for de Gaulle even if some never tired of (falsely) reducing him to the status of an aspiring despot.

As I have already stressed, de Gaulle was committed to keeping grandeur and moderation together, to doing full justice to both. In his first book, *The Enemy's House Divided*, which he began to research in prison libraries while a prisoner of war in Germany between 1916 and 1918, the future statesman explored the reasons for Wilhelmine Germany's defeat in World War I.[2] He admired the courage of the enemy but not its Nietzschean disdain for "the limits marked out by human experience, common sense and the law" that had permeated and corrupted German political and military culture before and during the Great War. At the beginning of the book, de Gaulle defended "a sense of balance, of what is possible, of measure" that "alone renders the works of energy durable and fecund." This was to become his political creed, his animating political philosophy: grandeur must be informed by realism, restraint, and *mesure*. It is at the heart of de Gaulle's greatness as a statesman and thinker.

In his subsequent interwar writings, as we have already had reason to discuss, de Gaulle expressed a mixed judgment about

---

2 The book was originally published in French as *La discorde chez l'ennemi* in 1924. An excellent English-language version, *The Enemy's House Divided* (a title with Lincolnian resonances to an American ear), translated, annotated, and with a most thoughtful thirty-eight page Introduction by Robert Eden, appeared from the University of North Carolina Press in 2002. It is one of the few books by de Gaulle that remains in print in English. All quotes from the book come from the "Foreword to the First Edition," pp. 1–3 in the American edition and are quoted in *JJ*, 54.

Napoleon Bonaparte. He admired his courage and military genius but faulted him for leaving "France smaller than he had found her." Napoleon had little appreciation for restraint, and like the German military elite in World War I, he was undone by "outraged principles," by the "tragic revenge of measure," as de Gaulle so eloquently put it in his 1938 book *France and Her Army* (quoted in *JJ*, 93).

The French conservative liberal Raymond Aron once feared "the shadow of Bonapartism," as he put it in a 1943 article, that surrounded de Gaulle and the Free French movement during their days of wartime English exile. But in 1958, after de Gaulle's return to power as the founder of the new French Fifth Republic, Aron differentiated the "classic 'Bonapartist' conjuncture" that paved the way for the general's return to power ("a climate of national crisis, the discredit of parliament and politicians, the popularity of a man") from any suggestion that de Gaulle aimed to be a new Bonaparte. As Aron framed it, Bonaparte was an "adventurer" and tyrant; Boulanger, who almost took part in a coup against the French Republic in 1889, was a "ditherer"; and Marshal Pétain, the hero of Verdun and leader of Vichy France, was "an old man." By contrast, de Gaulle was "an authentically great man" (*JJ*, 492). Those are the exact distinctions that needed to be made, and they are well borne out by Jackson's nuanced narrative. This distinction between Napoleon and de Gaulle, between a greatness that reluctantly acknowledges limits, if at all, and one that sees *mesure* as integral to greatness itself, is of paramount importance. As Patrice Gueniffey writes in his magisterial *Napoleon and De Gaulle: Heroes and History*, de Gaulle "always recognized that his action was delimited by values that transcended him: France and its history, his religious faith, the cause of civilization as opposed to that of barbarism, the rejection of tyranny or dictatorship."[3] In that sense, he was never a law unto himself. He exercised "commanding practical reason," as Pierre Manent has called it, true civic authority, but never succumbed to arbitrary rule. De Gaulle had the soul of a statesman and not an aspiring despot or tyrant.

The Edge of the Sword, de Gaulle's most famous work, written between World Wars I and II, took aim at a facile pacifism that ignored the harsh realities of a world where conflict formed an essential part of the life of nations. De Gaulle knew that the Great War, bereft of humane and prudent political leadership, had highlighted many of the horrors of armed conflict. But de Gaulle could not imagine a political world, a human world, "without force" (cited in *JJ*, 70). He did not glorify war and never endorsed conflict or imperialism as ends in themselves. Still, he asked in his preface to the book: "How can one conceive of Greece without Salamis, Rome without her legions, Christianity without the sword, Islam without the scimitar, the Revolution without Valmy?" (cited in *JJ*, 70). (Valmy was a French revolutionary battle well known to all French readers, at least in those days.)

A reader might ask: How did de Gaulle's opposition to pacifism cohere with his Christian faith? Like Péguy—and like the French Catholic novelist Georges Bernanos, whom he also admired—de Gaulle believed that the Christian, too, was called to the path of chivalry and personal and political honor. He was deeply Christian in other respects. De Gaulle viewed the condition of his daughter Anne, born with Down syndrome, as a trial from God. He loved her dearly and saw a humble greatness in "poor little Anne" (*JJ*, 63). He wept with terrible grief (he told the parish priest he felt "annihilated") when his daughter died at 20 in 1948. De Gaulle

---

3 See Patrice Gueniffey, *Napoleon and De Gaulle: Heroes and History*, translated by Stephen Rendall (The Belknap Press of Harvard University Press, 2020), 222.

told one of his aides in 1946 that Christ's sacrifice was at the center of universal history: "He opened up the horizons of religion beyond the hearts of men towards vast regions giving a place to human suffering, to human anguish, to human dignity" (*JJ*, 419–20). Jackson's de Gaulle is a *croyant*, a believer, whose personality, thought, and action were "impregnated" by his Christian faith (*JJ*, 23–26, especially 24).

At the same time, "the man of character," the model of political magnanimity that de Gaulle embodied and presented in Chapters Two and Three of *The Edge of the Sword*, was an ideal of heroic leadership marked by the most ascetic of stoicisms. (We will discuss this work in greater detail later in this chapter.) Jackson compares de Gaulle with Corneille's Augustus, a model of public service informed by solitude and some sacrifice of personal happiness (*JJ*, 17–18). No Nietzschean overman, de Gaulle suffered as only the "born protector" of a great and free nation can suffer. He was pained, as was Churchill, by Munich and the democracies' choice for dishonor and peace at any price. "Step by step," he wrote in the fall of 1938, the French had chosen the path of "humiliation and retreat so it had become a second nature" (Cited in *JJ*, 88). He would choose the path of personal and political honor, as a Frenchman, a Christian, and a good European. He had warned about Germany's bellicose intentions in the years after 1933 and pushed for the modernization of the French armed forces with new tank and air capacities that could take the war to the enemy. The French instead hid naively behind the ineffectual Maginot Line. There was more than a little moral corruption hiding behind this passivity, as de Gaulle persuasively argues in the first volume of his *War Memoirs*.[4]

4 See especially Chapter 1 ("The Slope") of *The Call to Honor* (*L'appel* in French) in *The Complete Memoirs of Charles de Gaulle*, translated by Jonathan Griffin and Richard Howard (Carroll and Graf Publishers, 1988), 3–52.

De Gaulle rose to the moment in June 1940. A terrible political, moral, intellectual, and military crisis called this "born protector" to lead a damaged France, at least that part of it that refused to surrender to a Germany far worse than the one of 1914. As Jackson observes, "without the fall of France, de Gaulle would undoubtedly have become a leading general in the French army, probably a minister of defense, perhaps even head of the government—but he would not have become 'de Gaulle'" (*JJ*, 122). De Gaulle, of course, was sensitive to the role of contingency, chance, and choice in the unfolding of human affairs, as all his writings suggest (the philosopher Henri Bergson was a key influence here). On these themes, Jackson quotes from one of de Gaulle's most insightful prisoner-of-war lectures in 1917:

> Without the Peloponnesian War, Demosthenes would have remained an obscure politician; without the English invasion, Joan of Arc would have died peaceably at Domrémy; without the Revolution, Carnot and Napoleon would have finished their existence in lowly rank; without the present war General Pétain would have finished his career at the head of a brigade. (cited in *JJ*, 122)

As Jackson emphasizes, in de Gaulle's view, Providence, destiny, and chance act as restraints even upon a "prince" filled with the capacity for truly effective thought and action. De Gaulle was an unusually reflective man of action, contemplative far beyond the capacities of most of his military and political contemporaries. He reflected quite seriously on questions that one can rightly call philosophical. Like Churchill, he knew that he was a "man of destiny" meant to leave his mark on history. The two statesmen were "shepherds" obliged to do battle with totalitarian "wolves." As

Jackson demonstrates, "word" and "deed" converged in the great "appeal" to honor and resistance that de Gaulle delivered from the BBC studios in London on June 18, 1940 (*JJ*, 3-4). A new "adventure," for de Gaulle, began at age thirty-nine as he observed early in his *War Memoirs*.[5] On June 18, de Gaulle reminded his listeners (and posterity) that the war was a global conflict. What was lost by mechanized force, the planes and tanks of the Axis powers, could be won in the future by the combined mechanized strength of the Allied powers. He knew that Britain and France could rely on their extensive empires and "the immense industry" of a United States that would be inevitably drawn to the cause of European liberty. He spoke simply but eloquently for French independence, for honor, and for the nobility of continued resistance. De Gaulle will always be remembered as the "man of June 18th," Jackson believes, even more than as the founder of the Fifth French Republic in 1958 (with its energetic, if distant and oligarchic, executive institutions) or as the statesman who reconciled France to the end of empire, if not to a radical diminishment of France's continuing "rank" in the world. But there is no doubt that he was pained by this very diminishment.

De Gaulle was not especially anti-American, as Richard Nixon and Henry Kissinger came to appreciate in the late 1960s. He worried about French and European dependence upon American military protection long before others became aware of this problem. He unhesitatingly sided with the West during the various Berlin crises from 1958 to 1961 and again during the Cuban Missile Crisis of October 1962. He may have been right about the imprudence of a long American military involvement in Indochina in the 1960s, but the man who warned Georges Pompidou in the

5 See the first pages of the chapter entitled "Free France" in *The Complete War Memoirs of Charles de Gaulle*, 81–83.

early 1950s about a potential "Asian Munich" might have shown more respect for American efforts to stymie the totalitarian tide. Were Ho Chi Minh and the Viet Cong merely nationalists, as de Gaulle suggested at Phnom Penh in 1966? Jackson establishes that de Gaulle genuinely hated Communism and did not like what he saw in the Soviet Union when he visited in 1944 and 1966 (*JJ*, 676-677). He thought, rightly as it turned out, that Europe would outlast a Communist ideology so at odds with human nature and the wellsprings of European civilization. But he was wrong in the 1960s in thinking that leaders such as Alexei Kosygin, Władysław Gomulka, János Kádár, and Nicolae Ceausescu were beginning to think and act like nationalists, even patriots. These men combined Bolshevism, no small dose of cynicism, and a lust for power. None was an authentic patriot, and none could be said truly to love his country more than ideology or the preservation of Communist rule. This was wishful thinking on de Gaulle's part, and Jackson is not sufficiently sensitive to this point (see *JJ*, 771). It goes too far to say, as Jackson does, that de Gaulle was somehow vindicated by the antitotalitarian revolutions of 1989.

As Jackson makes clear, de Gaulle was a traditionalist in his social leanings and sensibilities. He hesitated to legalize contraception (what would happen when marriage was just about sex and not at all about fecundity, he suggestively asked?), and he thought that the Catholic Church had gone too far in accommodating the excesses of the modern world in the aftermath of Vatican II (*JJ*, 711). He wondered, not without reason, if the Church still truly believed in the truths it professed. Yet he presided over the rapid economic modernization and cultural liberalization of France. As Jackson notes, when people think of postwar France, figures like Jean-Paul Sartre, Claude Lévi-Strauss, and Jean-Luc Godard come to mind, men who hardly shared de Gaulle's vision of French grandeur informed by moderation and respect for tradition (*JJ*, 770). And the student-driven events of May 1968 unleashed a radical assault on everything de Gaulle held dear.

Today, de Gaulle is an uncontested hero for the French, something he hardly was in his lifetime. Yet French elites owe much more to the secular antinomianism of May 1968, with its utter contempt for Gaullist austerity (moral and political), than to an authentically Gaullist vision. Emmanuel Macron, the current resident of the Élysée Palace, praises de Gaulle and claims that his *War Memoirs* provide continuing political inspiration. Macron undoubtedly loves the monarchical trappings of the French presidency, but he is hardly a partisan of the "greatness," "independence," and "rank" of France in the manner of de Gaulle. De Gaulle probably would be appalled by Macron's easygoing accommodation to the behemoth of the European Union and the dictates of a politically unaccountable Brussels Commission.

De Gaulle was an authentically great man, as revealed in his interwar writings, in his stoicism, in his passionate love for France, in his choice for honor and resistance in June 1940, and, above all, in the myriad ways he kept greatness and moderation together in his thought and action. But there were darker shadows too. De Gaulle often conveyed to his interlocutors an unnerving "mixture of melancholy and hubris" (*JJ*, 444–445). Jackson also reveals a man given to displays of anger, even rage, especially when France's liberty and independence were at stake or when he felt slighted as the preeminent representative of France's cause (*JJ*, 221). His austere character was accompanied by a puzzling willingness to use anger as an instrument of statecraft, as Churchill discovered. He was a noble if enigmatic figure, a good man but by no means a perfect one.

But his efforts on behalf of the independence and rank of France were somewhat Sisyphean, or so he came to think. De Gaulle even feared that he had amused his contemporaries with flags, as he told André Malraux in a final conversation, recorded in that writer's fascinating *Fallen Oaks* (cited in *JJ*, 758). Still, de Gaulle's writings and a stellar biography such as Jackson's provide enduring witness to a life lived in service to France and to the enduring verities that inform Western civilization. His ambition was at the service of something higher and deeper than his own self-aggrandizement, as I shall explain at greater length later in the next part of this chapter.

―――――

Friendship and the Solitude of Greatness

We now have a good sense of de Gaulle's achievement as a whole. Let us expose at greater depth the moral, intellectual, and spiritual sources of de Gaulle's "greatness." In decisive respects, he remains something of an enigma. A genuinely great man, at first glance, he seems to tower above mere humanity. In studying de Gaulle's biographies and writings, the statesman and military man eclipses the human being without leaving his human bearing wholly behind. De Gaulle himself emphasized the solitude and sadness that accompanied the burden of human greatness. Yet de Gaulle, the self-described "man of character," "the born protector," was also a loving husband, a not terribly demanding or severe father, a faithful Christian, and a French patriot. There were profound limits to his solitude and self-sufficiency. His austere magnanimity coincided with moderation, even benevolence. He loved his country, strove for greatness, and sacrificed something of his private happiness for the public good. He was a complex man and soul and perhaps a conflicted one, as I have already suggested.

A devoted family man, de Gaulle nonetheless was a man of few friendships. (I discuss the exceptions in the course of this presentation.) He was in no way an empty suit, a vacant soul. Still, he cultivated authority and prestige in no small part by remaining a mystery to those around him. What passions, thoughts, and feelings animated this enigmatic soul? This mystery cannot be completely dispelled, but it can be clarified with the help of de Gaulle's own self-presentation in *Le fil de l'epée* (*The Edge of the Sword*) and by attentiveness to key moments and episodes in his long and eventful life.

This tension between the public and the private, between greatness and the requirements of civility and affability, defines the figure we know as de Gaulle. (De Gaulle had a curious habit of referring to himself in the third person as de Gaulle, as if the private man, the real man, were separate, even distant, from the public persona.) Perhaps only Washington rivals him for the austerity, the seeming inaccessibility, of the man behind the public persona. Here we confront two great statesmen and military leaders, two authentically great men, moved by love of country, love of liberty, and the requirements of personal greatness. They share a stoicism, a rectitude, that is all too rare in a democratic age. But Washington, unlike de Gaulle, rarely lost his temper even if he was known to have a formidable one.

Democratic man in his contemporary form above all values authenticity, self-expression, and accessibility. He appreciates people who are "nice." He is not supposed to wear a mask, to keep part of his inner self hidden from those around him. And yet, paradoxically, there is something vacuous about these constant "democratic" displays of the "true self," which must be shared with the whole of humanity. The "true self" is often empty of substance, of spiritual depth, frequently contenting itself with the trivial or the commonplace. Such democratic displays are the opposite of Gaullist grandeur, which is inseparable from a certain hauteur.

De Gaulle did not have a democratic soul, but his humane version of magnanimity is needed by democracies, particularly in times of crisis. De Gaulle and Churchill were not wholly shaped by a democratic age. But their "quasi-aristocratic" virtues helped save European liberty in its confrontation with totalitarianism in the twentieth century. In Churchill's unforgettable Finest Hour Speech of June 18, 1940, and in de Gaulle's great "Appeal" to resistance of the same day, we confront powerful and eloquent appeals to personal and political honor at the service of helping to save a Western civilization that too often puts personal well-being above the old civic and military virtues. Churchill's and de Gaulle's contemporaries needed to be reminded of old truths (including the Roman virtue of courage) and the full range of the virtues.

As I have already stressed, one profoundly misunderstands de Gaulle if one sees in him an aspiring Bonaparte, a Caesarian figure threatening public liberties. He was quite critical (in *France et son armée* and elsewhere) of Bonaparte for severing greatness from moderation, for squelching public liberty, and for engaging in imperial overreach. De Gaulle was an egalitarian in two elemental but decisive senses: as a Christian he affirmed the dignity of man made in the "image and likeness of God" (and for this reason he opposed every form of totalitarianism), and as a French republican, he accepted civic equality as the basis of free, republican life. But he did not accept what might be called a democratic political psychology that affirmed human equality in almost every respect. Even democracies need statesmen, however much democrats delight in attacking inequalities and hierarchies as inherently unjust. De Gaulle believed that nature, human nature above all, is stronger than democratic ideology. Like Aristotle and Machiavelli (for all their considerable differences), he knew that there were a variety of human types. As to the question of command, the world was forever divided between the "great" and the "small" (on this point, see Book 3 of Aristotle's *Politics* and Chapter 9 of Machiavelli's *The Prince*). The great man must ally with the few or the many (or perhaps mediate their claims) and should not pretend that the human world is a homogenous or undifferentiated mass.

If men are "political animals," as de Gaulle asserts in *The Edge of the Sword*, they "feel the need for organization, that is to say for an established order and for leaders." This is not merely a matter of self-assertion on the part of the great as Machiavelli and Nietzsche might suggest. It is a matter of *justice* (as Aristotle suggests in his *Ethics*). A common or shared good is possible between the few and the many in a way that respects common decency, public liberty, and shared humanity. De Gaulle's great achievement as a statesman and political thinker was to meld together magnanimity and moderation or rather to show that the truly great man was a "born protector" and not a tyrant and a destroyer of bodies and souls.

The key to de Gaulle's self-understanding, to his unforced melding of magnanimity and moderation, can be found in the two central sections of *The Edge of the Sword*, on "Character" and "Prestige," respectively. Let us turn to those two revealing discussions.

The Man of Character

De Gaulle's account of "the man of character" in Part 2 of *The Edge of the Sword* (1932) is more than an account of "the virtue of hard times," as he calls it. It is nothing less than what André Malraux called an "anticipatory self-portrait." This anticipatory self-portrait allows us to see "de Gaulle" avant la lettre and thus to get a glimpse of the mysterious depths (as well as the self-understanding) that shaped his soul. De Gaulle's account of the "man of character" is at the same time an exacting self-portrait and an exercise in the political philosophy and political psychology (in the original, capacious sense of the term) that account for human greatness. Rarely has a statesman been so self-conscious about his own nature and motives and about the nature of the political whole (and the human world) in which he operates.

It is tempting—but mistaken—to give a Nietzschean interpretation of "the man of character." He is indeed an individualist who "has recourse to himself." One might think of him as a political artist who likes to act alone. "His instinctive response" to the challenge of events "is to leave his mark on action, to take responsibility for it, to make it his own business." His "passion for self-reliance" is "accompanied by some roughness in method." His subordinates initially groan under his command and are struck by his aloofness. The man of character knows that "there can be no authority without prestige, nor prestige" without personal distance. Hence, the austerity, the almost inhuman roughness, distance, and reserve that initially characterizes the man of character. It is hard to see how one can reconcile such a view of human greatness with an Aristotelian or Christian conception of a common or shared human and political good. But this is not the end of the story.

De Gaulle writes that "when events become grave, the peril pressing," things begin to change, and ordinary men turn to the man of character "as iron towards the magnet." The confidence of the "lesser man ('petits') exalts the man of character…and gives him a sense of obligation." He is no longer so solitary, so autarchic. He is moved by benevolence "for he is a born protector." The desire to protect, to give of himself, is deeply ingrained in his nature.

In other words, his soul is moved by generosity and not by the impulse to destroy or tear down in search of a field for his political ambition. He is a benevolent political animal in a community that he acknowledges as his own. He does not claim all success as his own even as he alone takes responsibility for failures. As I have argued in my book *De Gaulle: Statesmanship, Grandeur, and Modern Democracy,* de Gaulle's is an account of magnanimity marked by a Christian sense of benevolence and a classical appreciation of greatness of soul. As I have already argued in Chapter Two, Aristotle's magnanimous man does not display the same sense of obligation or generosity as de Gaulle's man of character even if his pride prevents him from committing injustice. He is virtuous, but he does not remember the good deeds of others. He is haughty, even contemptuous of lesser souls. He is not prone to admiration "since nothing is great to him" (*Nicomachean Ethics* 1125a, 2–3). For all his alleged haughtiness and austere distance, de Gaulle and his model of "the man of character" do not fit this description.

By contrast, de Gaulle's sense of personal and political greatness is profoundly marked by Christianity, by a deepening and a broadening of the soul's obligations to others. De Gaulle even calls the man of character the "good prince," a sure sign that the great French statesman had more than military greatness in mind when he published *The Edge of the Sword* in 1932. Just as a knight is moved by chivalry, by a mixture of aristocratic virtue and Christian obligation, de Gaulle's man of character eschews revenge and absorbs himself in salutary action for the common good. He is part of a larger moral and political whole. De Gaulle explicitly states that "justice appears" when the man of character is given his due. The "man of character" does not inhabit a world "beyond good and evil."

To reiterate: De Gaulle's man of character does not inhabit a Nietzschean world "beyond good and evil." Nonetheless, in the chapter on "Prestige," de Gaulle freely acknowledges the tension between Christianity and the political virtues. "The perfection preached in the Gospels does not lead to empire. Every man of action has a strong dose of egotism, pride, hardness, and cunning." This is undoubtedly also true of de Gaulle himself, who was not bereft of Machiavellian *virtù*.

De Gaulle's "hardness" was most obviously and disturbingly on display in his decision in 1962 to abandon the Harkis, the Algerian Muslims who had fought courageously and loyally for France in the Algerian War between 1954 and 1962, to their terrible fate (in many cases, imprisonment, torture, and death). De Gaulle undoubtedly wanted to bring the Algerian War to a quick end and to restore comity to France. But this abandonment of France's allies leaves a stain on the record of a man otherwise admirably devoted to national and personal honor. Still, de Gaulle's conception of the statesman as "born protector" surely owes as much to Christianity as to pagan antiquity even if the stateman qua statesman must eschew evangelical perfection. At the same time, the discussions of leadership in *The Edge of the Sword* undoubtedly express unresolved tensions in de Gaulle's complex soul.

Aloofness and the Melancholy of Superior Men

In the chapter on "Prestige," de Gaulle acknowledges a crisis of authority in the modern world. A statesman can no longer depend on the force of tradition or inherited institutions. In some profound sense, the old gods are dead or are at least tottering. De Gaulle was fully cognizant of what Walter Lippmann in 1929 called "the acids of modernity" three years before de Gaulle published his little book. Authority needs the support of artifice, and that means the cultivation of mystery, reserve, and aloofness on the part of a great military or political leader. De Gaulle recognizes that this is a very special burden, too much for many to bear. It demands "unceasing self-discipline, the constant taking of risks, and a perpetual inner struggle." Some great men buckle under these weights and withdraw from the austere demands of public life. The man of "reserve, character, and greatness...must accept the solitude which, according to Faguet, is the 'wretchedness of superior men.'" Tranquility and even friendship, certainly of the usual kind, are denied the man of character. An inchoate sense of melancholy surrounds him. De Gaulle reports a tale of somebody saying to Napoleon that an old and noble monument was sad. Napoleon's reply was revealing: "Yes as sad as greatness."

Is this de Gaulle's final word? Must the "born protector" choose a solitary life without family and friends? Is there an unbridgeable gap between the requirements of greatness and the requirements of human happiness? Or does de Gaulle exaggerate to make a point about the sacrifice of ordinary tranquility that sometimes accompanies personal and political greatness? In what ways did this particular man of character remain a human being, capable of tenderness, friendship, even Christian charity?

A Family Man

Before turning to the place of friendship in de Gaulle's public and personal life, it is necessary to say a word or two about the place of family in his affective life. Here his humanity is most clearly on display. His biographers, such as Jean Lacouture, Jonathan Fenby, and Julian Jackson, reveal a loving husband and father, a Catholic bourgeois who valued family ties and affections. He was in no way autarchic, self-sufficient, or anything resembling a god among men. He was a great man but very much a human being, as we have seen. His letters to his wife, Yvonne, are often affectionate and reveal nothing of a stern or uncaring *paterfamilias*. Theirs was a tie marked by love and affection as well as duty and responsibility. Even during the Free French years in London, de Gaulle had time for his family amidst his grave political and military responsibilities. He was proud of his son Philippe's service in the Free French navy (he went on later in life to become an admiral) and wrote Philippe an affectionate letter to that effect. In his letters, he was always "papa" or "affectionate papa," and if he was not conspicuous with affection in person, neither was he cold and stern with his children. (Lacouture records a tender grandfather at Colombey-les-Deux-Églises during the final years of his retirement who enjoyed taking walks with his grandchildren Anne Boissieu and Yves de Gaulle, Philippe's second son.) He even laughed, and laughed heartily, on occasions. The country writer, as Lacouture calls him (he was completing his *Memoirs of Hope*), and tender grandfather is eminently human and humane and is in no way of another essence. He is seemingly at home with himself and with others.

The Faithful Christian

As I noted earlier in this chapter, the French military officer and statesman had a special relationship, one marked by deep and abiding love, for his daughter Anne, who was born on New Year's Day 1928 with Down syndrome. She was to live twenty years and is buried at Colombey-les-Deux-Églises with Charles and Yvonne de Gaulle. She brought out the best in de Gaulle as father, husband, and Christian. Fenby, Jackson, and Lacouture all describe de Gaulle's enormous devotion to Anne: the only word the girl managed to say properly was "papa." He played with her after returning from work, kissing her, singing songs, and allowing her to play with his military cap. He would take her for walks in the botanical gardens in Metz before World War II and would rock her gently for an hour or two at a time before she fell asleep. The little girl loved him in her own way.

The Catholic writer Henri-Daniel Rops, a friend of de Gaulle's before the war, reports a moving discussion he had with de Gaulle in which he confided the "heavy cross" that he and his wife had to bear because of Anne's unfortunate condition. But they never thought for a moment of putting Anne in an institution. As Fenby points out, de Gaulle's character may have been decidedly stoic, but with Anne he found a "blessing" and his "joy." This same man who went to mass at a French church in London every day during the war responded like a Christian who paradoxically found joy in his suffering and in the love it brought forth for Anne. As Lacouture reports, his friend, the Catholic writer André Frossard, observed that there was more love in the world because of Anne. De Gaulle welcomed the trial of Anne's diminished condition and suffering also as a gift that encouraged him "always to aim higher" (as he once was overheard saying by one of her doctors). He famously remarked upon her death that "now she is like all the others." It is hard not to see grace at work in this loving encounter between a wounded child and her loving father. In de Gaulle we see no Nietzschean contempt for the weak, the disabled, the suffering. The "man of character" is indeed a "born protector" and in this case even an exemplary Christian.

A Paucity of Friendships

If de Gaulle was surrounded by a loving family, if great joy arose even from the "trial" that was Anne's life, it cannot be said that his was a life rich in friendship. Fenby reports that in Trier in Germany, where de Gaulle was stationed in the late 1920s, he stayed after work to fraternize with his young junior officers. He discussed history with them. Nothing personal, nothing intimate. He stood apart, both because of his height and because of his self-command (which Fenby falsely reduces to "ego," a characteristic modern reductionism). One witness to these encounters observed de Gaulle's "extraordinary loneliness." This observer asked, "Beyond his excursions into history, what could the [then] major say? Who could he talk to? What about?" The "man of character," it appears, does not converse about commonplaces. Like Aristotle's "magnanimous man," he preoccupies himself with high and noble things and perhaps even his own deeds. He is difficult to bear and somewhat "rough in his methods." His greatness undoubtedly sets him apart. Solitude is part of his condition even if, as I have shown, it is not the only or final word.

But what about friendship with other statesmen, with those rare few imbued with a sense of human and political greatness? For all their disagreements in the course of the war, for all his sense that Churchill and England had taken advantage of "wounded France," de Gaulle clearly admired Churchill. In the famous description in Volume 1 of the *Mémoires de guerre*, Churchill appeared to de Gaulle "from one end of the drama to the other, as the great champion of a great enterprise and the great artist of a great history." There could not be higher praise from de Gaulle. He brilliantly describes Churchill's unparalleled ability to "play upon" the "angelic and diabolical gift" of politics and political rhetoric "to rouse the heavy dough of the English as well as to impress the minds of foreigners." Churchill was "a man of destiny" (in his own words), or in Gaullist terms "a man of character." Churchill and de Gaulle never became friends, at least in the fulsome sense of the term, but they admired each other and never allowed frictions in the relationship between their two nations (or between Free France and Britain) to ultimately undermine that mutual respect and admiration.

Could a relationship between two magnanimous men, two great "men of character," ever be free of friction and misunderstanding? That seems unlikely. The historian François Kersaudy has told the story well. One of the first things de Gaulle did upon returning to power in 1958 was invite a very old and frail Churchill to Paris to be honored by the French government and nation. And from Churchill's own death in 1965 until de Gaulle's in November 1970, de Gaulle wrote Clementine Churchill every January on the anniversary of Churchill's death. Unlike Aristotle's magnanimous man, de Gaulle had a gift for seeing greatness in others. He was capable of genuine admiration. As a conservative in the best sense of the term, he appreciated what Churchill had done to protect Europe and the West against the scourge of totalitarianism. Both men never severed greatness from moderation or lost an appreciation for the dignity of what de Gaulle freely called "les petits," those with no aptitude for leadership or command. As I have noted, Churchill and de Gaulle are best understood as "shepherds," born protectors, who were never tempted to become totalitarian "wolves." This is a distinct human type, the "magnanimous man" marked by moderation and solicitude for the common good of his country. Lincoln, too, belongs to this category.

Malraux, the "Inspired Friend"

There was one public man whom de Gaulle called his "inspired friend." In a luminous passage in his *Memoirs of Hope*, he speaks of André Malraux, always sitting to his right, an "inspired friend" and "devotee of lofty destinies." Malraux, the great novelist, adventurer, theorist of art, and longtime Gaullist minister of culture, gave de Gaulle "a sense of being insured against the commonplace." Malraux's own sense of greatness fortified de Gaulle, and his "flashing judgments would help to dispel the shadows." De Gaulle had often expressed friendship and esteem for Malraux. But Malraux feared that de Gaulle primarily saw him as a symbol who lent intellectual credence to Gaullism. Malraux thus doubted if the general truly thought of him as his friend, as his equal. Nonetheless, Lacouture reports that Malraux was elated to read the aforementioned passage in de Gaulle's final set of memoirs and "dashed off at once" to read it aloud to his friend, the great antitotalitarian writer Manès Sperber. It must also be recognized that de Gaulle bestowed his final intellectual testament to Malraux, recorded in that great dialogue between the poet and the statesman that is *Les chênes qu'on abat, Fallen* (or *Felled*) *Oaks*. Here, de Gaulle expresses his deep concerns about "the crisis of civilization," if not his final despair about France and his legacy. As I noted in the first part of this chapter, the great French statesman, departing from public office, feared that he amused his fellow countrymen by waving flags, as he puts it in a particularly pointed formulation. It is a recreated encounter or conversation but one "based on profound truth," as Lacouture rightly observes.

De Gaulle and Malraux were never intimates. But a lofty vision of France and civilization united them as well as a refusal to rest content with the commonplace. Theirs was a friendship marked by a common dedication to a "politics of grandeur" and a shared sense of de Gaulle's own indispensability to France and the West. De Gaulle does not use the word "friend" lightly. We must then respect his judgment about Malraux as revealing an essential truth. And still, this friendship was in decisive respects austere and distant, as befitting the quasi-solitude of "the man of character."

Adenauer and de Gaulle: A Great Political Friendship

There is one statesman whom de Gaulle called his "illustrious friend," Konrad Adenauer, the chancellor of West Germany between 1949 and 1963. The two men met in France and Germany fifteen times between de Gaulle's return to power in 1958 and Adenauer's departure from office in 1963. They also corresponded on more than forty occasions. They came to admire each other and developed a personal friendship that accompanied and helped deepen the political and spiritual reconciliation of France and Germany in the period between 1958 and 1963. As François Kersaudy has noted, de Gaulle admired Adenauer for his intransigent opposition to Hitler and National Socialism before and during World War II and for the independence he displayed in dealing with the British occupation forces in Germany after 1945. In Adenauer, de Gaulle saw a man of immense personal integrity, a German patriot (but not a deranged nationalist), and a statesman of the first order. Adenauer was at first suspicious of de Gaulle, fearing that he was a virulent nationalist who opposed European integration and who was insensitive to the Soviet threat. His first encounter with de Gaulle at Colombey-les-Deux-Églises cured him of any misgivings. De Gaulle's nationalism was much more moderate and humane than Adenauer had anticipated. The two great men saw eye to eye on the key issues of the day, and both were firmly committed to an enduring rapprochement between France and Germany.

Adenauer was profoundly touched by the fact that he was welcomed at de Gaulle's home in the fall of 1958 as a member of his family and was struck by the simplicity—and naturalness—of de Gaulle's manners and personal bearing. The two men developed an authentic friendship that was sometimes clouded by differences on geopolitical matters (de Gaulle was suspicious of what he saw as West Germany's excessive deference to American leadership, and Adenauer was worried, wrongly in retrospect, that France was indifferent to the Soviet threat to Berlin). But these bumps in the road never led to anything like a break or an undermining of the mutual respect in which each statesman held the other. Kersaudy goes so far as to say that a "great friendship" developed between these two remarkable statesmen in the years between 1958 and 1963.

Adenauer came to France on a state visit in July 1962, where de Gaulle welcomed him as a great German, a great European, and a true friend of France. Two months later, de Gaulle traveled to Germany, where he was met by rapturous crowds and where he delivered fourteen sterling speeches in exquisite German (his biographers report that he worked exceedingly hard to perfect these speeches). He displayed what Kersaudy aptly calls the "Gaullist magic." Of course, the capstone of Franco-German reconciliation was the signing of a treaty of friendship between the two nations on January 2, 1963, a reconciliation that was symbolized by these two Catholic statesmen coming together for prayer in the cathedral of Rheims, a city much contested in previous Franco-German wars and conflicts. Kersaudy notes that Adenauer was a cold man and de Gaulle an eminently proud one. Yet both believed that the "deeds of friendship," both personal and national, could in this case replace the "miseries of war," as de Gaulle strikingly put it in his *Memoirs of Hope*.

Adenauer died on April 19, 1967, not without a touch of sadness as he confronted the isolations of extreme old age and the loss of political responsibilities. But as Kersaudy notes, he had told de Gaulle four years earlier that "the personal friendship" between the two men was "one of the very rare presents" that he took away from political work. For his part, de Gaulle told aides that Adenauer was the "only one that I am able to consider as my equal." Churchill's powers and influence were by now long eclipsed (he died at the age of ninety in January 1965). He was alive but no longer on the world stage. And political—and national—differences (particularly regarding the centrality of the partnership with the United States) prevented their mutual admiration from being transformed into sustained personal friendship. However, with Adenauer and de Gaulle, we see how two world-class statesmen—committed in their own ways to humane national loyalty, opposed to every form of totalitarian domination, and deeply devoted to the Christian sources of the European spirit—could bury the past to build a future on new and more solid foundations. Along the way, a personal friendship developed between two proud if eminently decent and humane men.

Conclusion

We have explored the complexity of Charles de Gaulle's soul and self-understanding. His "anticipatory self-portrait" in *The Edge of the Sword* allows us to see how benevolence and solitude coexisted in this great man's soul, combined with some "roughness in method." This "born protector" was not a Nietzschean "Overman." He loved his family, cared deeply for his country, and felt a sense of obligation toward those who looked to his protective leadership. A Christian and a man of honor, he believed in justice and the common good and did not act as if "God is dead." He was a loving husband and father, and his deliberately cultivated austere public persona did not crowd out human feelings and tenderness in the family realm. In dealing with his beloved daughter Anne, he suffered like a true Christian and even found joy and consolation amidst a great trial. He was a man of few friendships and does not seem to have experienced the kind of virtue-friendship, the joint perception of the good (*sunaisthesis*), that Aristotle describes in the ninth book of his *Ethics*. He appeared to many who knew him as arrogant and distant. This was not merely a flaw of character. De Gaulle knew that in an age where character, in the specifically Gaullist sense, depended on the cultivation of "prestige," some sacrifice of human intimacy must be made by the "man of character." He also knew that this sacrifice was for the common good. He undoubtedly felt sadness and loneliness but also love, affection, tenderness, and pride for self and country. His friendships with Malraux and Adenauer are particularly telling. De Gaulle was an authentically great human being and statesman, not just a "charismatic leader," to use the desiccated language of our official social science, which can no longer talk about the highest human types or about any souls for that matter. And the great French statesman was remarkably reflective about his own soul and activity.

Sources and Suggested Readings

Julian Jackson's *De Gaulle*, translated by Steven Rendall (The Belknap Press of Harvard University Press, 2018), stands out among all the biographies of de Gaulle, in any language, for its comprehensiveness, its clarity and elegance, its careful attentiveness to de Gaulle's thought as well as his action, and its ability to do justice to both the "greatness and the misery" of de Gaulle and the Gaullist enterprise.

De Gaulle's self-conscious melding of greatness and moderation is nowhere more apparent than in his first book, *The Enemy's House Divided*, translated, annotated, and with an introduction by Robert Eden (University of North Carolina Press, 2002). First published in French in 1924, this lucid book of political history (and political philosophy) defends "classical rules of order" and the respect for common sense, human limits, and human experience that inform them against the extreme Nietzschean overvaluation of energy, audacity, and human willfulness.

I have drawn freely on sections two and three ("Character" and "Prestige") of Charles de Gaulle's *The Edge of the Sword*, translated by Gerald Hopkins (New York, NY: Criterion Books, 1960), 35–78, especially 41–44 and 55–66. This elegant but inexact translation should be checked against the French original, *Le fil de l'epée et autres ecrits* (Paris, France: Omnibus/Plon, 1994). For example, on page 44 of the English translation, the crucial phrase "bon prince" ("good prince") disappears.

For a fuller discussion of de Gaulle's portrait of "the man of character," see Daniel J. Mahoney, *De Gaulle: Statesmanship, Grandeur, and Modern Democracy* (New Brunswick, NJ: Transaction Publishers, 2000), 41–66.

On de Gaulle's family life and the relationship with Anne de Gaulle, see Jonathan Fenby, *The General: Charles de Gaulle and the France He Saved* (New York, NY: Skyhorse Publishing, 2012), 89–91 and 159–65 and Jean Lacouture, *De Gaulle: The Rebel: 1890–1944*, translated by Patrick O'Brian (New York, NY: W. W. Norton, 1990), 107, and *De Gaulle: The Ruler: 1945–1970*, translated by Patrick O'Brian (New York, NY: W. W. Norton, 1992), 578. Julian Jackson also more than competently treats all those matters.

For the fascinating account of de Gaulle's relationship with the other officers at Trier, see Fenby, 89.

For De Gaulle's magisterial description of Churchill, see *The*

Complete War Memoirs of Charles de Gaulle (New York, NY: Simon and Schuster, 1967), 57–58.

For the beautiful passage on Malraux, see Charles de Gaulle, *Memoirs of Hope: Renewal and Endeavor*, translated by Terence Kilmartin (New York, NY: Simon and Schuster, 1971), 272. For Malraux's reaction to this passage, see Lacouture, *De Gaulle: The Ruler: 1945–1970*, 584. For the inspired final conversation between de Gaulle and Malraux, see Malraux, *Felled Oaks: Conversation with de Gaulle* (New York, NY: Holt, Rinehart and Winston, 1972) and the discussion in Lacouture, 584.

See pages 173–81 of the *Memoirs of Hope* for de Gaulle's own account of his emerging friendship with Konrad Adenauer. The phrase "illustrious friend" is used on page 181. I am indebted to François Kersaudy's excellent article "De Gaulle et Adenauer, aux origines de la réconciliation Franco-Allemande" on the website of the Institut Charles de Gaulle.

Communism was overthrown by life, by thought, by
human dignity.

—VÁCLAV HAVEL,
Summer Meditations (1992)

Genuine politics—politics worthy of the name, and the only
politics I am willing to devote myself to—is simply a matter of
serving those around us: serving the community, and serving those
who will come after us. Its deepest roots are moral because it is a
responsibility, expressed through action, to and for the whole, a
responsibility that is what it is—a "higher" responsibility—only
because it has a metaphysical grounding: that is, it grows out of
a conscious or subconscious certainty that our death ends nothing,
because everything is forever being recorded and evaluated
somewhere else, somewhere "above us", in what I have called "the
memory of Being"—an integral aspect of the secret order of the
cosmos, of nature, and of life, which believers call God and to whose
judgement everything is subject. Genuine conscience and genuine
responsibility are always, in the end, explicable only as an expression
of the silent assumption that we are observed "from above", that
everything is visible, nothing is forgotten, and so earthly time has
no power to wipe away the sharp disappointments of earthly failure:
our spirit knows that it is not the only entity aware of these failures.

—VÁCLAV HAVEL,
Summer Meditations (1992)

The epigraphs to this chapter come from the opening chapter ("Politics, Morality, and Civility" of Václav Havel, *Summer Meditations*, translated by Paul Wilson (New York: Vintage Books, 1993), pp. 4–6.

$$=== 8 ===$$

VÁCLAV HAVEL:
WRITER, DISSIDENT, AND
PHILOSOPHER KING

The definitive biography of Václav Havel by Michael Zantovsky, *Havel: A Life*,[1] makes clear that Václav Havel is the
closest thing to a philosopher-king the late modern world has experienced even if Havel had little final power as Czech president.
Let us follow the path thoughtfully and gracefully prepared by
Zantovsky in order to enter into Havel's considerable achievements as writer, thinker, dissident, and statesman.

Zantovsky, a long-time friend and sometime press secretary to
Václav Havel, went on to become Czech ambassador to Washington and to the Court of St. James in London. He has intimate
knowledge of Havel. He freely admits to "loving" Havel (Z, 6–7)
even as he maintains his critical distance and avoids anything
resembling hagiography. Zantovsky is aided in this seemingly
impossible task by his experience as a clinical psychologist, which
allows him to combine admiration with detachment and remark-

---

1 Michael Zantovsky, *Havel: A Life* (New York: Grove Press, 2014). All citations are noted parenthetically in the text as *Z* followed by the appropriate
page number.

able descriptive powers. Unlike so many other critical accounts inspired by suspicion and anti-elitism, his "loving" but measured account leaves Havel's greatness undiminished.

As Zantovsky shows, Havel was "one of the more fascinating politicians of the last century" (Z, 1) even as he was much more than a politician. He ably explores Havel's multiple roles as writer, dramatist, moralist, dissident, and anti-totalitarian theoretician. The book also captures Havel's myriad "contradictions," which were never too far from the surface. A born leader who was kind, polite, humorous, and self-effacing, he was also a "bundle of nerves," prone to depression and self-medication as well as to "sometimes ill-considered sexual adventures" (Z, 3). Havel's admirers are obliged to confront that latter point. This moralist did not readily apply moral criteria to affairs of the heart and was sometimes promiscuous in ways that belie conventional morality and religious principles. He seems to have at least partly bought into the radically "individualist" ethos of the 1960s, at least as regards "personal" morality. Zantovsky provides an insightful analysis of the Czech dissident culture of the sixties and seventies, which was in most respects admirable even as it defended sexual "freedom" as a venue for individual autonomy in an order dominated by totalitarian repression and the erosion of individuality.

Sexual indiscretions aside, Havel was an intensely spiritual man who didn't adhere to any religion. Despite his admiration for Pope John Paul II and his prison friendship with the future cardinal archbishop of Prague, Dominik Duka, he "did not die a Roman Catholic" (Z, 13). But he respected religion and even attended secret masses in prison. In his voluminous writings and speeches, he upheld a quasi-theistic "conception of being" and an understanding of "responsibility rooted in the memory of Being" (see the second epigraph at the beginning of this chapter). In Havel's philosophical conception, everything we do is remembered, "recorded," by "Being" itself. This was Havel's equivalent of immortality; it provided cosmic grounds or support for moral responsibility. These spiritual convictions, deep and penetrating yet sometimes bordering on New Age philosophy, were a staple of Havel's speeches at home and abroad during his years as president first of Czechoslovakia and then of the Czech Republic.

Much of Zantovsky's book traces Havel's remarkable partnership with his wife of many years, Olga Hávlova. Their relationship was both solid and stormy. Olga was Havel's "rock." A strong and capable woman who acted as his editor and first reader, she was his eyes and ears at home and during his four periods of imprisonment. Havel was frequently unfaithful to her and she, too, was less than faithful to him. Yet a larger fidelity, an unbreakable partnership, undergirded Havel's serial infidelities. For her part, Olga was loyal *and* fiercely independent. Havel's imprisonment in the early 1980s gave rise to his most philosophical work, *Letters to Olga*,[2] a work combining high-order philosophical reflection with sometimes obnoxious instructions and advice to his wife. Olga knew how to handle Havel's more tyrannical requests. She later served

2 See Václav Havel, translated by Paul Wilson, *Letters to Olga* (London: Faber and Faber, 1990). As Paul Wilson notes in his Introduction to the volume (p. 17–19 in particular), the last sixteen letters in the book are profoundly philosophical and are intended "to be read as a unit." Human beings are "thrown" into the world but nonetheless experience "Being in the I" (Letter 133, p.333). They are free to pursue "the lost fullness of Being" (letter 135, p. 337) or to succumb to the temptation to make themselves gods, which is the path of "self-enslavement" (p. 339). Havel limns the path of moral and metaphysical "responsibility" (p. 34) versus the path of fanaticism, where "the love of truth, freedom, and justice" is replaced "with the love of an ideology" (Letter 141, p. 364). Havel is ambivalent about whether Being is God (Letter 137, p. 346), but he freely identifies Being "in its subjective aspect" with "infinite memory, an omnipresent mind and an infinitely large heart" (p. 346).

as a faithful first lady who nonetheless kept her personal distance. She comes across as a woman of immense strength, her dignity on display in her stoical confrontation with terminal cancer in the 1990s. By contrast, Havel's second wife, Dagmar, guided him through many health crises but was preoccupied with celebrity culture and was not nearly as beloved by the Czech people.

Zantovsky's book is not primarily about Havel's thought, though it gives an expert and reliable account of the principles that guided his thought and action. Its treatment of his seminal 1978 essay "The Power of the Powerless" is superb. Havel's genius was to locate the specific features of the "post-totalitarian regime," ideological to the core but no longer relying on mass violence in the manner of a classic Leninist-Stalinist regime. Like Solzhenitsyn before him, Havel saw the ideological lie as the glue holding together a totalitarian or post-totalitarian regime. The green grocer who thoughtlessly raised the sign "Workers of the World Unite" above his produce stand was "ritualistically" reinforcing the hold that the regime of the lie had on human souls.[3] The spiritual decision "to live in truth" could break the lie's ritualistic stranglehold and open up a space for personal integrity, human rights, and even a nascent civil society. The "power of the powerless" lay precisely in the ability of truth to break through the "automatism" of the lie. It was the Achilles' heel, the unique point of vulnerability, of a seemingly invulnerable totalitarian order.

The Czechoslovakian dissident movement pursued the path of truth with Charter 77, a courageous document that called upon the authorities to live up to obligations agreed to in the 1975 Helsinki accords and even in Czechoslovakia's mendacious Marxist-Leninist

3 See "The Power of the Powerless" in Havel, *Open Letters: Selected Writings: 1965–1990*, selected and edited by Paul Wilson (New York: Alfred A. Knopf, 1991), pp.125–214. See pp. 132–34 for the famous discussion of the green grocer and his revolt against the tyranny of ideological clichés.

constitution. Its original signatories were few, but they spoke for the self-respect of a submerged civil society. Its spokesmen, such as Havel and the great Czech philosopher and phenomenologist Jan Patočka, were men of undeniable courage and integrity. Their movement was informed by solidarity, dignity, and resistance to the lie. Patočka had considerable influence on Havel's subsequent thought and action. In his memorable essay "What Charter 77 Is and What It Is Not," Patočka discussed the difficulty of sustaining moral responsibility in modern, technological civilization, of which totalitarianism was the caricature and perfection. He defended the "unconditional nature of Principles" that are for all intents and purposes "sacred" (Z, 182). He knew that salvation could never come from the state. Havel was deeply moved by Patočka's death after repeated interrogations by the STB, the Czech secret police, in 1978. Havel, too, felt compelled to act when confronted by the "unconditional character" of "sacred" principles. Repression—and another prison sentence—quickly followed.

Havel was convinced that modern technological civilization did not have the moral resources to sustain itself and was undergoing a crisis. This led him to have some sympathy for the Greens and other countercultural movements. Yet he had no sympathy for pacifism, peace movements, or unilateral disarmament. In his 1985 essay "The Anatomy of a Reticence," he discusses the asymmetry of Western pacifists and Eastern dissidents and critiques the moral blindness of the 1980s peace movements, which didn't understand the nature of totalitarianism and were committed to unilateral disarmament that Havel saw as a "disingenuous form of suicide." As Zantovsky suggestively puts it, "sometimes one could only live in truth by taking up arms" (Z, 437). In his presidential years, Havel opposed every form of appeasement, supported intervention in Kosovo (though he failed to appreciate all the complexities of that situation), and gave moral support to the overthrow of Saddam Hussein (though Havel had some reservations about how this was pursued). Zantovsky speculates that Havel never received the Nobel Peace Prize because of his principled opposition to appeasement and pacifism.

Zantovsky also sheds light on the *annus mirabilis* of 1989, part revolution, part ideological implosion, and part negotiated transfer of power to Havel and his political movement, the Civic Forum. The Czechoslovakian people rediscovered the tools of civic life and the courage to oppose ubiquitous lies. Havel's New Year address of January 1, 1990, spoke about a "contaminated moral environment"[4] as he promised not to lie as previous governments had habitually done. Havel, following Tomáš Masaryk, Czechoslovakia's first president, invoked Jesus and the power of trans-political principles rather than Caesar and power as ends in themselves.

There were difficult days after 1990. The split between the Czech Republic and Slovakia left the Czech people with a moral hangover. Havel did his best to appeal to the better angels of their nature when he became president of the reconstituted Czech Republic in 1993. But his power was diminished, and he exercised influence primarily through moral suasion. Zantovsky exposes the silliness of those who complain that Havel was some kind of leftist or Jacobin in his years in office. Havel was no utopian; the existential "revolution" he called for had nothing to do with violent, revolutionary, or totalitarian politics. His philosophical themes were often conservative or anti-modern (though never in a reflexive or irresponsible way).

One of Zantovsky's major contributions is to shed some light on the famed dispute between Havel and Václav Klaus, Havel's principal rival for moral and political preeminence in the post-Communist Czech Republic. Klaus is often caricatured as a "soulless,

4 See "New Year's Address" in *Open Letters*, pp. 390–96, especially p. 391.

cynical technocrat" and Havel as a "leftist" and "do-gooder" (Z, 456). Klaus defended the market, economic freedom, and allegiance to the "national community as the conduit of history, culture and traditions" (Z, 456). He was a Eurosceptic of the first order and a critic of radical environmentalism. Havel emphasized solidarity, tolerance, human and minority rights, care for the environment, and civic activism. Havel was distrustful of Russia; Klaus distinguished between the totalitarianism of the Soviet Union and the more moderate authoritarianism of Putin's Russia. Yet Zantovsky suggests that the two men had more respect for each other than they would admit. Both were anti-Communist. Klaus acknowledged Havel's historical role and his contribution to the Czech Republic's international reputation. Contrary to legend, he was also a cultivated man. And Havel knew he would not have become president in 1993 without Klaus's support.

After his political career ended, Havel was not seen as a prophet in his own country—until his death in 2011, when he was "rediscovered" by his countrymen. Zantovsky beautifully describes the mix of joy and mourning that accompanied Havel's death and funeral. He calls it the "joy of being confronted with greatness" (Z, 14).

Zantovsky's book shows us genuine human greatness and the fragility of even the most admirable human being. The writer and statesman who "played a prominent role in putting an end to one of the most alluring utopias of all times" (Z, 1) also reminded us of the indispensability of civility, grace, courage, and responsibility in a postmodern world that increasingly mocks truth and greatness.[5] Havel's irony, so evident in his fiction, never counte-

5 Havel's principal rival as a "freedom fighter" in the late twentieth century is undoubtedly the now better-known (especially among the young) Nelson Mandela, the anti-apartheid activist who became the first president of a multiracial South Africa in 1994. Mandela, who today is the subject of something resembling hagiography, spent twenty-seven years in prison on Robben Island,

nanced cruelty or disdain for truth or the moral life. Havel is, in important respects, the model of a humane, liberty-loving "philosopher-king."

"To the Castle and Back": Reflections of a Philosopher-Statesman

In February 2003, Václav Havel stepped down as president of the Czech Republic, having served two terms in office and an earlier, incomplete one as leader of the now dissolved Czechoslovakian state. It was an event of real significance. The dramatist-turned-dissident-turned-statesman remained the only figure of note in the region whose political position and moral authority spanned both the momentous anti-totalitarian revolutions of 1989 and the everyday challenges of post-Communist politics.

---

off Cape Town, after leading the banned African National Congress toward sabotage and selected violence as the instrument of choice to combat the cruel and unjust policy of apartheid or enforced "racial separation" in South Africa. Mandela's (and the ANC's) turn toward violence and a close alliance with the South African Communist party will continue to be legitimately debated. *The Prison Letters of Nelson Mandela*, edited by Sahm Vetter (New York: W. W. Norton, 2018) and his autobiographical *Long Walk to Freedom* (New York: Hachette Book Group, 1994) reveal a tough-minded, disciplined, and genteel man navigating difficult and demanding personal and political matters. He was in no way thuggish or personally prone to violence, and his personal bearing impressed even some of his white prison guards. Released from prison in 1990, he had the prudence, good sense, and grace to negotiate (in conjunction with South African President F. W. De Klerk) a peaceful transition toward a post-apartheid regime. As president of South Africa, he prevented violent recriminations and gave his considerable moral authority to the cathartic process represented by the Truth and Reconciliation Committee. A great man in certain respects, he nonetheless had considerable blind spots. Mandela did little to stop the massive corruption within the ruling ANC party. And he continued to esteem oppressive left-wing tyrants such as Fidel Castro, Muammar Gaddafi, and Robert Mugabe who had supported the "liberation" struggle.

In a compelling (if somewhat eccentric) work *To the Castle and Back*,[6] Havel recounts his role as a sometime "fairy prince" in the peaceful events that brought down Communism. He also provides a fascinating account of his efforts as a democratic statesman presiding over the decommunization of his country and its entry into the community of free nations.

With the fall of Communism, Havel entered a new phase in his life, setting the tone for morally serious civic engagement in a newly democratic society. This proved no easy task. Czechoslovakians had been deeply corrupted both by totalitarian mendacity and by the compromises they had felt compelled to make with the Communist state during the harsh "period of normalization" that followed the crushing of the Prague Spring of 1968.

As Havel made clear in earlier works, such as 1992's *Summer Meditations*, he saw his new political role as fully consistent with his dissident opposition to totalitarianism. In his post-1989 books and speeches, Havel continued to defend a moral vision of politics that he called "nonpolitical politics" or "politics as morality in practice." The epigraphs to this chapter perfectly reveal Havel's philosophical and spiritual commitment to genuine politics as a "responsibility expressed through action," to a "higher responsibility" with a distinct "metaphysical grounding." For Havel, the Good is ultimately not unsupported. He identified this vision with the demanding but liberating task of "living in truth." In all the aforementioned writings, Havel refused to identify politics with a dehumanizing "technology of power," the notion that power is an end in itself. Instead he defended a moral order that

6 Havel, translated by Paul Wilson, *To the Castle and Back* (New York: Alfred A. Knopf, 2007). All quotations will be cited internally as *C* followed by the page number in the volume.

stands above law, politics, and economics, a moral order that "has a metaphysical anchoring in the infinite and eternal." His speeches as president, many collected in English in *The Art of the Impossible* (1997),[7] were artful exercises in moral and political philosophizing, enthralling Western audiences even if Havel tends to repeat himself.

Havel was a partisan of "personal experience" but never of subjectivism and relativism. His 1984 address "Politics and Conscience,"[8] written to be delivered at the University of Toulouse upon receiving an honorary doctorate (Havel was, of course, banned from traveling at the time), provides his most satisfying account of the ground of moral judgment. He appeals to the "natural world," or *Lebenswelt*, the world of personal experience where "categories like justice, honor, treason, friendship, infidelity, courage, or empathy have a wholly tangible content, relating to actual persons and important for actual life." Being, or the Absolute, "grounds, delimits, animates and directs" the life world. To revolt against its requirements and demands, its limits and obligations, is to succumb to arrogance and *hubris* and inevitably has "cruel consequences." For Havel, "wholly personal categories like good and evil still have their unambiguous content and, under certain circumstances, are capable of shaking the seemingly unshakable power with all its army of soldiers, politicians, and bureaucrats." In the end, ideological despotism stands naked before "the phenomenon of human conscience."

But Czechs began to tire of their "fairy prince." Havel's opponents in the press and the political class ("the snide brigade,"

7 Václav Havel, *The Art of the Impossible: Politics as Morality in Practice, Selected Writings and Speeches, 1990–1996*, translated by Paul Wilson and others (New York: Alfred A. Knopf, 1997).

8 See "Politics and Conscience" in Havel, *Open Letters*, pp. 249–71, especially pp. 250–53, 255–56, 270–71.

[*C*, 179], as he calls them) increasingly dismissed him as a naive "dreamer," a mere moralist with zero relevance to the pressing challenges of a post-Communist era. Abroad, Havel continued to be widely admired as a hero and moral witness; at home, those enamored of a more pragmatic or technocratic view of politics dismissed him—and all the dissidents of old—as "left-wing" curiosities who somehow had very little to do with the collapse of Communism. I have already commented on this strange but convenient distortion. This dismissal of the historic importance of the dissident resistance to Communism no doubt assuaged the consciences of those who did nothing to fight totalitarianism before 1989.

To the Castle and Back defends "nonpolitical politics" as a realistic response to the dilemmas of post-Communist politics—and modern politics more broadly. For the cursory reader, the unsystematic character of the work might be confused with something thrown together, a substitute for a carefully crafted memoir. In fact, as James Pontuso has argued,[9] Havel has structured the book with great care. He combines an extensive interview, conducted with the Czech journalist and broadcaster Karel Hvizd'ala, detailed notes to his staff between 1993 and 2003, and a "postpresidential" diary, written in three different locations.

Underscoring his artful weaving together of these literary forms, Havel tells us that he significantly modified Hvizd'ala's questions to the point of treating him "a little like a dramatic character in one of my plays" (*C*, 244). The interview—always interesting, sometimes confrontational, ranging from the gossipy to the philosophical, as much self-interrogation as interview—is the

9 James F. Pontuso, review of *The Castle and Back*, *Society*, January/February 2008. I am indebted to Pontuso in particular for highlighting the specifically literary and philosophical character of Havel's memoir.

book's core, providing its thematic and narrative unity. "It is no accident," as the Marxists used to say, that Havel's apologia centers around a defense of the soundness and efficacy of his core moral idea of nonpolitical politics.

In the course of the extended dialogue with Hvizd'ala, the reader comes to appreciate how ludicrous it is to reduce Havel to the label "left-winger," a point I already made in the opening part of this chapter. Havel may have had an instinctive liking for the Lou Reeds and Frank Zappas of the world—he clearly identifies with the anti-totalitarian "spontaneity" of rock and roll music—and for a long time he found a home in the *bien-pensant* pages of *The New York Review of Books*. But Havel also reveals himself as an eloquent defender of the market economy, a critic of the indifference of prosperous peoples to those suffering tyranny or genocide under totalitarian regimes, an enemy of appeasement and pacifism, and a friend of dissidents in Cuba, Belarus, and China. He was a conservative-minded ecologist, a qualified multiculturalist who rejected moral relativism, and a defender of taste and civility in a mass society. In fact, the unreconstructed left regularly denounced him as a man of the right.

Responding to his critics on the right—represented above all by the Civic Democratic Party of Václav Klaus, Havel's principal rival and detractor in the 1990s and his successor as president of the Czech Republic—the old dissident points out the subterranean bonds connecting "market fundamentalists" who ignore the moral foundations of the free society with their Communist enemies (*C*, 157–59). In their facile dismissal of moral imperatives and their reduction of politics to an essentially economic problem, they perpetuate some of the core pathologies of the totalitarian left, Havel believed. They confuse his anti-totalitarianism with an indulgence for the left, when in fact it reflects a deeper philosophical perspective on modernity, one that can be called "postmodern" in the limited sense of seeking to go beyond the philosophical premises underlying modernity. In decisive respects, it transcends the dichotomy between left and right, something Havel's more fevered and superficial Czech critics could never understand.

Consider Havel's evocative comparison of politics and drama. Dramatic or literary art, Havel writes, attempts "to deal with [the] fundamental amorphousness of life, to uncover something like the structure of Being, to display in vivid terms its internal weave, its hidden structure, and its real articulation" (*C*, 277). Too often politics appears as a "strange, never-ending process with no clear turning points and no unambiguous and immediately recognizable outcomes" (*C*, 277). In the modern world, politics can "appear to be hopelessly boring, a gray, dull administrative grind, enlivened occasionally by a scandal or pseudo-scandal that is forgotten as soon as it is over" (*C*, 278). Without succumbing to irrationalism, Havel attempts to awaken his readers to the "structure of Being," of responsibility and choice grounded in the order of things, that underlies even prosaic political life. His memos and diary entries jump from period to period in an effort to reveal the underlying connections and "real meaning" of political life that a one-sided emphasis on "mechanical chronology" covers over. Whether laboring over a speech, describing his efforts to restore and beautify the centuries-old "Hradčany," or Castle—the historic seat of government in Prague—or preparing for trips abroad, Havel alerts his readers to the nontechnocratic aspects of politics: the importance of taste and civility; the inescapable role of personal considerations, including friendships among statesmen (Havel counted a pope, the Dalai Lama, and former American secretary

of state Madeleine Albright as friends (*C*, 146, 199, 339–40));
and beauty as an elevating corrective to the reductively mechanical expressions of modern civilization.

A quiet sadness informs Havel's artful philosophical memoir.
True, Havel never loses sight of life as a precious gift or of his
time in office as an opportunity to face new challenges and to
defend his principles. We see him subjected, however, to endless
calumnies, struck by illness and facing the death of his beloved
first wife, Olga, and the widespread castigation of his second
wife, Dagmar ("Dasa") Veskrnová, for no other reason than she
was an assertive woman who wasn't Olga (an equally assertive
woman, as we have seen, *C*, 252–56). Instead of writing new plays
and books, Havel struggles to write speeches and feels haunted
by the sense that he is endlessly repeating himself (to which there
is some truth as I have already suggested). The reader experiences precious time lost, the approach of death, the self-doubts
of this "man of paradoxes," as he has been called, all too human
in his weaknesses and contradictions.

By the book's conclusion, we leave behind the "fairy prince"
and discover—or rediscover—the artist, philosopher, and statesman. If Havel delighted too much in the company of vapid
celebrities such as Robert Redford and Sharon Stone—did anyone ever tell him that they actually admired the Fidel Castro
whom Havel despised?—and if he too readily resorts to New
Age symbolism, he still exemplifies those intellectual and spiritual qualities integral to human freedom and dignity. *To the
Castle and Back* shows how philosophy, literary art, and statesmanship met in the thought and action of a true anti-totalitarian
hero and titan. There was nothing in the end utopian about his
affirmation of "politics as morality in practice." As Havel argued
in *Summer Meditations*, the morally serious student of politics

knows that "heaven on earth" will never be and that efforts to attain it lead to nothing but tragedy and suffering. Havel was a self-described moralist "without illusions."[10]

Sources and Suggested Readings

Michael Zantovsky's *Havel: A Life* (New York: Grove Press, 2014) will remain the definitive account of Havel's life for a long time to come. James F. Pontuso's *Václav Havel: Civic Responsibility in the Postmodern Age* (Lanham, MD: Rowman & Littlefield Publishers, 2004) remains the best account of the recovery of the pre-theoretical "natural world" that underlies Havel's thought, writing, and statesmanship. David Gilbreath Barton's *Havel: Unfinished Revolution* (Pittsburg: University of Pittsburgh Press, 2020) is a useful account for a less specialized reader looking for a basic overview of Havel's thought and life. But it lacks the intimacy and intellectual depth of Zantovsky's work.

The philosophical core of Havel's thought is best expressed in the opening chapter of Havel's *Summer Meditations* (New York, Vintage Books, 1993), "Politics, Morality and Civility," pp. 1–20. Havel's foundational essays such as "The Power of the Powerless" and "Politics and Conscience" can be found in Havel, *Open Letters: Selected Writings: 1965–1990* (New York: Alfred A. Knopf, 1991).

Havel's memoir *To the Castle and Back* (New York: Alfred A. Knopf, 2007) perfectly bridges his literary, philosophical, and political concerns and illumines the challenges of recovering free and decent politics in the post-Communist world. It is his last great "dramatic" work and a testament to his idiosyncratic, artful, and morally serious brand of philosophical statesmanship.

10 Havel, *Summer Meditations*, pp. 16–17.

A FINAL WORD

In important respects, the writing of this book has entailed nothing less than an act of intellectual and moral recovery, and a most welcome one at that. The intellectual clerisy in the West—and that includes myriad demi-educated academics, activists, and journalists—is increasingly committed to the negation or repudiation of our civilizational inheritance. We have come face to face with a new *logocracy*, as the Polish Nobel Laureate Czesław Miłosz called it in *The Captive Mind* in 1953, a tyranny founded on the manipulation of language and the forced imposition of ideological clichés with little or no connection to anything real or enduring. As I have noted in this book from time to time, angry and ignorant mobs demand the cancellation of the most notable and noble figures in our tradition, and statues of the great and good have fallen or have been effaced throughout the United States and to a lesser extent in Great Britain too. They began by demanding the removal of Confederate statues but soon toppled statues in a lawless and truly indiscriminate way. In the summer of

2020, in response to the killing of George Floyd in Minneapolis, buildings burned, statues of heroes were toppled, "cancellations" multiplied, and ideological indoctrination became the order of the day. A new Manichean racialism was rigorously enforced in our schools, media, corporations, churches and, indeed, through nearly every institution of civil society.

The political class either cheered the chaos, mayhem, and institutionalized self-loathing demanded by those who repudiated America and the West in principle (the left) or stood by in stunned silence (most on the right). One very imperfect man, Donald J. Trump, spoke up and spoke up well in defense of the country, most notably at Mount Rushmore on July 4, 2021. But, as everyone knows, he lacked the self-discipline, the rhetorical precision, the self-control, and the liberal learning to be a true statesman. Still, in his bones, he saw the culture of repudiation and the "political correctness" that informed it for what they were at a time when no genuine statesmen were in sight. Trump could boast and exaggerate with impunity, as he did almost every day. But as the journalist Lance Morrow has pointed out, his opponents often told and continue to tell ontological lies: that Trump was a Russian agent and protofascist; that he organized and led an "insurrection" on January 6, 2021, the day of the lamentable and dangerous breach of the Capitol; that Communism is worthy of a serious reconsideration; that America is irredeemably and "systematically racist"; and that human beings can reinvent their sexuality at will by choosing among 153 (and counting) arbitrary "genders." The left has hypocritically and inconsistently become fixated on "the assault on truth" (ideologically defined) after promoting moral relativism and postmodern "deconstruction" of the true, the good, and the beautiful for fifty years or more. Trump is no one's "beaux ideal of a statesman" (to quote Lincoln's famous words about Henry Clay in 1852). But nor was he a dangerous, incipient tyrant. In the name of fighting untruths and "fake news," massive new lies proliferate. And the Big Tech companies have become agents of repression.

Let me say a word about Ronald Reagan and Margaret Thatcher, the two greatest statesmen in the Anglo-American world in the last half century, a man and a woman of unimpeachable character, unlike the chaotic Trump. Neither were statesmen-thinkers in the elevated and capacious sense I have explored in this book. Nor were they precisely "great-souled" in the classical meaning of the term. But they were inspired "conviction" politicians who were dedicated to good, even noble, principles and ideas. They understood, truly understood, the threat that Communist totalitarianism posed to both humanity and Western liberty and did their best to educate public opinion to that effect. They presided over the denouement of the Cold War with a combination of tough-mindedness, prudence, and grace that allowed the self-implosion of Soviet Communism to proceed apace. Reagan's great speech before the British parliament on June 8, 1982, boldly rejected the idea that Communism would last forever and was somehow historically inevitable. At the heart of Communism, Reagan insisted, was a radical denial of "human freedom and human dignity." Reagan fully appreciated that Communism was both *contra naturam* and doomed to near-term self-destruction.[1] He clearly and seemingly effortlessly saw what the cognoscenti could never see.

Thatcher shared these convictions and stood up nobly for Britain's sovereignty and the liberty of the British subjects on the

---

1 See "The Crusade For Freedom," address to the British Parliament, London, June 8, 1982, in *The Last Best Hope: The Greatest Speeches of Ronald Reagan*, Introduction by Michael Reagan (West Palm Beach, FL: Humanix Books, 2016), pp. 98–105.

Falkland Islands when those islands were attacked by the Argentinian dictatorship in an act of naked aggression on April 2, 1982. Her resolve to defend and recapture the Falklands, faraway islands in the South Atlantic, was characterized by an indomitable Churchillian resolve. Thatcher also forcefully defended the justice, morality, and efficiency of the market economy against every form of statism and collectivism. But contrary to legend, she was no soulless libertarian. Her defense of fair and lawful economic initiative and competition was accompanied by a high-minded defense of the rule of law and the "vigorous virtues and values," as she memorably called them, of courage, determination, and responsibility to both one's country and those in one's care. The British prime minister was also a thoughtful Christian who championed the enduring relevance of the Judeo-Christian inheritance to the exercise of human freedom and responsibility. She unapologetically defended national sovereignty and a vision of Europe wider and deeper than the transnationalism championed by contemporary advocates of the European project in its present form, most famously in a speech delivered in Bruges on September 20, 1988. After leaving office, she even said, in a speech on September 19, 1992, that if she were a Frenchwoman, she "would rally to the General's standard," de Gaulle's that is, "and cry, *Vive l'Europe Libre!*" By that she meant a Europe of cooperating but independent and self-respecting nations. She was that most unusual thing: a Gaullist-Atlanticist.[2] (De Gaulle, in contrast, favored French participation in NATO in 1949 but

2 I have drawn on *Margaret Thatcher: The Collected Speeches*, edited by Robin Harris (London: HarperCollins, 1997), pp. 308–14, pp. 315–25, and pp. 550–51 and on John O'Sullivan's *The President, The Pope, and the Prime Minister* (Washington, DC: Regnery Publishing, 2006). O'Sullivan rightly emphasizes "the spiritual element that best explains" Reagan's and Thatcher's lives and achievements. That spiritual element is sorely lacking on both the left and right today and does much to explain our current crisis.

removed France from the military wing of NATO in 1966, believing that it promoted European subordination to and dependence on the American superpower.)

Let us return to the heights. Cicero was indisputably right that magnanimity tempered by moderation—noble statesmanship informed by liberal learning, applied political philosophy, and high prudence—is among the best ways of life available to human beings (along with the life of contemplative reflection, the dedication of one's life to reflective and prayerful service to God, and the writing of literature open to moral realism and the apperception of the grandeur and misery of the human soul). A "culture of repudiation," as the late, great Roger Scruton called it, thus wars with the noblest manifestations of human nature and civilized existence. It remains our obligation to reaffirm the real in a spirit of gratitude for what has been passed on by our forebears as a precious gift. We can again see the likes of the great statesmen-thinkers chronicled in this book if we dare to repudiate repudiation and once again open ourselves to human excellence in all its forms. To fail to do so would be a brazen act of nihilism and cowardice at the service of pure negation. The choice is ours.

INDEX

Page numbers followed by n indicate notes.